The Fabulous 40 & Over Club

MIKI RILEY

DEDICATION

To All Who Truly Want To Be Fabulous!

CONTENTS

INTRODUCTION

Like many of us, have you ever wondered how life would be when you got older? Where would you be living? How would you be living? What would you be doing for a living? Would you be married or have children? What places would you have traveled to? Would your current friends still be in your life? And etc…

I can't speak for everyone but I'm pretty sure the feeling and opinions I type down in this book will be understood by many. Why, because as the Bible says, "there is nothing new under the sun". The life experiences many of us encounter have been encountered by someone previously time and again. There may be slight variations, but the stories will still be similar time and over again. How each person reacts to varying circumstances can many times change the course of their life for good, bad, better or worse. Most people instinctually react similarly to comparable circumstances.

Prime example, some think the Bible is so outdated, but a story sticks out in my mind that reminds me of similar stories I've heard of over time. This young lady who had several brothers kept hanging with the girls in a neighborhood outside of where she grew up. Of course, this was against the advice of her family. The girls she was hanging with were raised with different values than hers. I'm sure she thought there was no harm in what she was doing. She got close with one of the most popular guys in the neighborhood she visited. Well the Bible says he "defiled" her. It's my assumption that means he raped her. How else did her family find out? If she wanted to have sex with him and it was against her custom, do you think she would have told on herself? Put yourself in that scenario, you take a liking to what seems like an interesting, friendly guy. After a while you either fall in love with him (or so you think) one thing leads to another and you end up having sex. Do you go and blab that to your big brothers and your parents? I surely say the typical answer would be "no."

Or the scenario could have been while hanging out with your girlfriends frequently, you get to know this guy who seems pretty cool. As a matter of fact, you kind of like him, you may have even given him a hug or a kiss and he decided he wants it all, and he takes it against your consent. Now you tell your family. Why? Because he "defiled" you. You weren't ready to give it up. You may have wanted to save that for the man you planned on marrying. Well I'm pretty sure that was what Dinah had in mind. Oh, and by the way this is my rendition of the story of Dinah as told in the book of Genesis in the Bible. Dinah's brothers were furious! So much that they plotted and not only killed the man who had sex with her but also his family and friends.

Maybe you haven't heard this exact story but I'm sure you've heard of someone or group being retaliated against by the family member of a girl that has been raped.
The question is, could this situation have been prevented by either party taking a different course of action, or even heeding the advice of someone more mature? Or, could the reaction have been handled differently so as not to have affected so many lives? This is just one of the reasons why I'm writing this book. There is someone out there who has encountered things similar to what you have or have yet to encounter. They have words of wisdom, advice and possible encouragement that you can use which could actually affect the outcome of your life in a positive way, should you take heed.

Most people who are in their 20's and 30's feel as did I, that by the time they are 40 they will be more established and settled in life, experienced and mature. That is the case, most times. However, each person is different.

When I was in my early 20's I always said my ideal age was 40. Of course, I had to get pass the teenage years, just wanting to be legal enough to have a drink in the club or not having to be worried about being carded at the liquor store. Why? Because liquor is so important when you aren't old enough to legally consume it for some reason.

My teenage years didn't come and go fast enough. Why? I guess, because I thought I was grown for as long as I could remember thinking, and my mother did her best to burst my bubble every chance she got. I can just remember the childish looking dresses and shoes she'd make me wear to Bible study. I'd be so upset and embarrassed. I remembered she'd make me uncross my legs during the sermons and I'd be so irritated with her. I couldn't understand what her problem was. Looking back, I couldn't have been more than about 6 or 7 years old. I only know this because of where we were living during the time. I only lived on Hamlin Street during the ages of 5 and 11 years old and this nonsense (or so I thought at the time) was going on well before we moved.

I was the girl who told strangers I was 16 when I was really 12. I loved wearing makeup at a young age. My mom didn't approve, but any chance I got to put my hands on some mood lipstick as soon as I left home for school, you know what it was. The dark pinker the lips the better, it made me look older and more mature, or so I thought.

I left home for what I thought would be for good at the age of 17. I thought it was then that I started my journey to Fabulousness...

What we define as Fabulousness at an early age can actually affect the outcome of our lives. How, you might ask and what does this have to with anything I previously mentioned? We'll analyze this together as you continue reading...

CHAPTER 1

WHY THE WORD FABULOUS

Let's start by discussing where the word fabulous comes from. According to my research, the word derives from fable. What is a fable? A fable is a fictitious tale or a short story, typically with animals as characters, conveying a moral lesson like a parable.

An example of a parable is the camel and the needle.

"It's easier for a camel to get through a needle's eye than a rich man to get into the kingdom of God." *Matt 19:24.*

Now we know ain't no Camel getting through the eye of a needle. That's just a fantastic story for the purpose of emphasizing the need to stay focused on God's kingdom.

Fables are fantastic stories, and fantastic is just one of the words used in the Merriam Webster's thesaurus to describe the word Fabulous. Merriam Webster's definition of the word Fabulous is
1: resembling or suggesting a fable: of an incredible, astonishing, or exaggerated nature.
2: wonderful, marvelous, attractive, interesting, fascinating, famous and fantastic.
Other words related to the word fabulous according to the thesaurus are fake, false, feigned, fabricated, fictional, fictitious, fanciful, imaginary, imagined, made up, make-believe, pretend, unreal and mythological.

Also fabulous of old meant dull, boring, tiring, uninspired and worrisome.

Now which words or definition would you like to be associated with? Incredible, astonishing, wonderful and marvelous or fabricated, fictitious, make-believe and unreal or uninspired?

As mentioned earlier, what we define as Fabulous can actually shape the future of our lives. How you may ask?

As a little girl you were molded as to what to think is

pretty. Think about it... What did your mother tell you was beautiful? How was your home/bedroom decorated? How were your dolls dressed? How did your mother dress you? What colors did she put you in? How were you told to act? What was acceptable and unacceptable? What made you think that your mom, your aunt, your grandmother, was super beautiful? What did you think in your mind you would do just like them?

Good Example of shaping my definition of Fabulous:

As a young girl, I always admired my aunt Mildred. When she would come visit the family, she always had on stiletto heels, big curly hair and long manicured polished fingernails. I always said to myself *"I'm going to have pretty fingernails just like my aunt when I grow up."* To this day, my fingernails are long, oval, manicured and polished like I always promised myself, just like aunt Mildred's wore.

My aunt was also an entrepreneur. She was an articulate, hard-working woman who took pride in what she did and how she looked. In my childhood I did not see that. I saw the fingernails and the hair and the heels. All of which cost money to maintain. I didn't see the hard work behind the outward beauty.

At a young age being pretty on the outside was always important to me. I was really into what I was wearing, how I was wearing it and making sure my hair was on point. There are a few things however that really shaped my future and I did not realize it until later in life.

When I was around 15 years old, I was talking to my mom in the kitchen while she was cooking. She asked me, *"So Miki, what type of business will you have?"* I really thought about it in that moment. My response was to have a cleaning company. My mother told me to write my business plan out that very moment. How was I going to execute my plan? Detail by detail I wrote out how I'd make my cleaning company a success. She asked me challenging questions which helped me think out my plan to execute my business plan successfully.

At the age of 16 I started a cleaning company. I was my only employee, however, I had accounts and making money. I washed towels for a of beauty salons and I also cleaned homes in my neighborhood. I was proud of my accomplishment. And to this day I'm proud to say I had my first business at the age of 16. I have been an entrepreneur ever since.

This introduction into entrepreneurship shaped my life and had even more of an impact on me than making sure my nails would stay pretty, just as I saw my aunt's.

Bad Example of shaping my definition of Fabulous:

As a young girl, maybe as far back as three years old, I remember my father doing my hair and taking me to school as well as picking me up. My siblings and I would see my mother in the evening's after work and on weekends. It was then that she would prepare dinner and my father would always be served first. If we were having fried chicken, he would get the biggest and the best (so I thought at the time) piece, the breast. There would be times that I would serve him his plate if she was still preparing in the kitchen.

Having an involved and supportive husband and father is always a good thing. But over the years I noticed that my father would not keep a steady job. My mother was always working long hours outside of the home (until she became an entrepreneur herself and had a home-based business) leaving my siblings and I to fend for ourselves until the evening when she would return. My mother appeared to be the breadwinner of the family. My father went from being home to only showing up in the evenings and disappearing on the weekends. She would get angry, they would argue but after all was said and done my father seemed to still be treated like a king (so I thought).

This affected my future decisions in the men I chose to be a part of my life and marry (yes, it's been a few times) as well is what I allowed to take place in my own relationships. What I eye-witnessed somehow shaped what I felt was acceptable. Not valuing my self-worth or even knowing how. Knowing your self-worth and loving yourself is an imperative 1st step to understanding what true Fabulousness is.

These are just a couple of examples that show even the little things in life can shape you. What you admire and value now, and in the past, as being Fabulous can have a real impact on your future definition of Fabulousness.

CHAPTER 2

WHAT'S SO SPECIAL ABOUT 40

The number 40 is mentioned 146 times in Scriptures, it generally symbolizes a period of testing, trial or probation.[1]

Walter B. Pitkin wrote a best-selling novel in 1932 called "Life Begins at 40". This phrase was coined from that point on. The life expectancy back then was only around 60 years old. It was thought we didn't reach full maturity until the age of 40. This would only have given a person about 20 years to live their best most Fabulous life. But things have changed. Forty is no longer considered old. We're living now close to 100 years old or more.

---

[1] https://www.biblestudy.org/bibleref/meaning-of-numbers-in-bible/40.html

Now let's analyze this for a moment. There are a few women I can think of that we all know who appear to be living their best lives well over 60 years old. The first person that comes to my mind is Tina Turner. A few years ago, I was trolling through Facebook and I saw a video with Beyoncé and Tina Turner singing her famous song, "Proud Mary." I tell you, Tina Turner looked so good, she was moving up and down the stage with her Fabulous legs! This woman looks like she's barely aged. I remember looking at her videos as a young girl. "What's Love Got to Do with It" (in my best singing voice). And she was singing before I was born. Tina Turner is still Fierce and Fabulous.

There's Tina Turner, Diana Ross, Cher, Chaka Khan and of course Oprah Winfrey just to name a few women who seem to be living great lives past the age of 60 years old.

Angela Bassett, who is now 60, still looks as young and in fit as when she portrayed Tina Turner and "What's Love Got to Do with It". I've personally admired her and it seems like she looks even better with time. She's married, has twins and every time I see her in her interviews on TV she looks so pleasant, peaceful and Fabulous!

So, I've named some in their 70's and 60's who are still Fabulous. Here's an example of someone in their 50's who's still looking Fabulous and appears to be living their best life. Janet Jackson ("Miss Jackson if you nasty", Ha!). This woman just had a baby at 50 years old! Janet Jackson has been performing ever since she had her baby and her body looks Fabulous. You've got to do nothing but assume she's eating right, working out and living her best most Fabulous life.

Now to the 40's. Jennifer Lopez ranks high on the list of women in their 40's who is looking more than fabulous at her age. Jennifer Lopez is at the top of her game. I just saw one of her videos, her body looks amazing. I need her skin regimen secrets because it doesn't look like her skin is aging at all.

If I had a chance to interview some of these Fabulous ladies, I would ask one question: *"What is your definition of fabulousness."* Although they look more than beautiful, I'd be willing to bet that they believe being fabulous is much more than the pictures we see of them.

These are just a few examples of people we all have seen to be healthy and living great lives past their 40's and beyond. I'm happy to say we're not living in that era when people were dying young.

Now, let's get back to the number 40.

According to Sandy Nubauer's article, "There are 10 reasons why life begins at 40." [2]

#10 *"Your 40's are no longer a fashion wasteland."*

She talked about how bad middle age versus youthful dress attire was back in the day. Back in the 80's young people dressed like Madonna, lace gloves leotards, headbands, lots of fake jewelry and teased hair. Because parents wanted to look visibly different and more mature than those outlandish styles, they went overboard in the wrong direction. Middle-aged people really looked old based on their dress.

How I relate to being past my fashion wasteland period is, I remember those days when I'd wear anything or almost nothing, now I see the wisdom behind the phrase "leave something to the imagination". It's my opinion that old saying is still valid today.

---

[2] Nauber, Sandy https://www.listland.com/10-reasons-life-begins-40/ March 2, 2017

#9 *"Modern knowledge and technology help us stay young."*

With the latest skincare products and surgical procedures mature women have been able to freeze their looks so that they look younger longer. No one was talking about Botox back in the 80's, however it does wonders especially when used in the right amounts. There are also less invasive nip and tuck's that some use to keep their faces lifted and bodies tight.

#8 *"Your children are out of diapers!"*

Many of us in our 40's have either grown children or almost grown teenagers. Even if you're like me and you end up having one in your 30's, they have an older sibling that can be with them should you have to get up and go. You are no longer running around after babies and changing diapers. You've now got more time to do you.

#7 *"But you can have more if you want them."*

That's right, you are still young enough to have kids if you want them. With todays medical advancements, it is a safer process. If you feel like you are still in the baby making mood you can still go for it!

#6 *"Your sex life starts to really get steamy."*

Studies have shown that women hit their sexual peak in their late 30s-40's. Women in this age range tend to more secure with their bodies and their relationships. This gives them the freedom to explore every side of their sexual nature.

#5 *"You are more financially stable."*

For most people by the time you've reached 40 you are somewhat settled into the job that you will retire from. You have acquired more experience and savings over time being in your long-time employment. However, that is not always the case. Sometimes you find that you are tired in your settled job and decide to step out on faith and become entrepreneurs or small business owners. This can lead you into a new chapter of Fabulousness for your 40s and beyond.

#4 *"You have worked out who are your real friends."*

In your 40's your friends have been in your life for quite some the time. In most cases, years. Because you've aged together, you've been through thick and thin, child births, death of family members, graduations and all kinds of celebrations. They are your real friends because they've stood the test of time.

#3 *"You have learned that aging is better than the alternative."*

Because of time and experience, you're kind of glad you've gotten past the unreasonableness of your youth. Think back to all the stupid things you did when you where young and all of the unnecessary trials and tribulations that could have been avoided if you had more experience.

#2 *"You have learned to be kind to yourself."*

There is nothing like learning to take care of yourself. How can you take care of someone else if you aren't in good physical and mental health? For example, when on a plane you are instructed to put the oxygen mask one yourself first before you can help someone else. Imagine being oxygen deprived while trying to help your child, it doesn't work. Sometimes it takes a long time to learn this fact.

#1 *"You know who you are!"*

Yes, it takes a long time to learn who you really are. When you're young, your life goes through phases. You change because of learning from certain experiences. Around the age of 40, you begin to settle into yourself.

Going back to my first quote, the reason why it was thought maturity was not reached until the age of 40 is because it takes that long to learn from tests, trials and probation. Think about it, those who are 40 and over, we've done some of the same things over and over again until we learned from them. Our thinking ability didn't mature until we were resolved to get serious about life. And that doesn't seem to happen most times until we are nearing the top of the hill.

CHAPTER 3

GENERATIONS AND THEIR DIFFERENCES

People are so different these days. I can remember going to the hairdresser (that's what they called cosmetologists/hair stylist back in the day) every other week or when my mother could afford to get my hair done. She took me to the same hairdresser she went to. My mom went to her to get her hair done for years. It wasn't until her hair came out with some Jerry curl method that she stopped going to this woman. I can't think of her name for anything. But I sure remember her face and how that beauty shop looked where she worked on Division near Pulaski out West in Chicago.

Most people back then went to the same hairdresser for years. There would have to be some serious falling out, either of the hair or a bad argument to cause a person to stop going to the same hairdresser.

Those of us in the same age range understand this devotion because we still go to the same stylist we've been going to for years, that's if we are still getting our hair done professionally.

That's just one example of what I call loyalty. That word seems to be extinct these days. People these days flip-flop to whoever is popular at the time. And you get what you pay for. Just because someone comes around saying they can beat your stylist's price by $20 doesn't mean they're going to do as good of a job as your stylist has been doing for so long. No one seems to know what loyalty is these days. Why?

My contemporaries and I (those of us who around the same age and older) find common ground in discussing the matter of how different young people are today as opposed to the 70's, 80's and even early 90's.

Talking about differences, when our young women used to date, we were taught that chivalry was not dead. It was the expectation that the man would treat, especially on the first couple of dates. And the women weren't giving it up so quickly, at least that we knew of.

Even back in the 90's, guys would try to help the woman they were dating in whatever way they could. Not as much today. Some men (or should I say males, not men) want and expect you to take care of them. Why, because so many women are taking care of men. These days women are so easy to give up their resources, love and money that many of our young and older men have stopped stepping up, because they don't have to!

This reminds me of Isaiah's prophecy, it says at Isaiah 4:1 about a time when seven women will grab a hold of one man and say *"...we will eat our own bread and we will wear our own clothes, just let us be called by your name."*

Now, I'm not saying that a man should do everything for woman, especially for someone he just met and for no good reason. Nor am I saying that a woman should not help her man. What I am saying is, I agree with what the Bible says: *"...a man that does not provide for his own household is worse than a person without faith."* 1Timothy 5:8. Let's keep in mind that it says *provide for those who are his own*. This means that if he is not claiming you and/or you have not solidified your relationship in the eyes of God, it does not apply to you (just something to think about).

From Karen P. L. Hardison enotes article[3], she commented on the differences of how people think now as opposed to in the past. This is some of what she had to say: *"One great difference between thinking then and now is that then, the majority of people thought of themselves and of others as bound by moral strictures whereas people today don't think themselves bound in the same way."*

She went on to say, *"As a small example, in the past, generally speaking, having the door of a home closed was enough to keep intruders out (generally speaking) while today even a bolted door won't keep them out since they feel no hesitation in breaking windows or anything else to gain their goal. The fear of going out of moral and legal bounds that kept a certain kind of order in Western society has dissipated and declined throughout present-day society (think of mass school shootings and mass shopping mall shootings)."*

This is so true! What bound us once, no longer has value in most people's eyes today. When a person does not have moral integrity or accountability, they are capable of anything. This is why people are

---

[3] https://www.enotes.com/homework-help/whats-difference-between-thinking-people-past-408852

willing to darn near scratch out your eyeballs in a sense to move you out of their way. This can happen due to jealousy, envy and a competitive spirit.

Examples:

1. If a woman sees a married man, let's say your husband, and she even knows he's your husband, she doesn't care. She's willing to do whatever it takes to get him away from you. Why? Because she wants him for herself. She doesn't care if it's going to break up your family or cause your children to lose out on a present father. Oh, and adultery, who even knows or cares what that means these days. She has no moral compass.

2. Someone makes an appointment with you at your business. You confirm the date and time. They don't show up or call, and you see them on Facebook out on a lunch date during the same time they scheduled their appointment with you. Their word has no value.

3. You go to Walmart because you need to pick up some things for your family and your household. You're at the checkout counter when the cashier tells you your debit card payment has been declined. You call your bank and your account has been emptied. You have zero funds. Why? Because someone has

committed fraud on your account. They've used all your funds by getting your account number and created a bogus credit card and went on a shopping spree. To make things worse they're probably one of your Instagram or Facebook friends that's posting up a super fantastic, fraudulent and fabled picture with the brand-new custom-made outfit and Gucci purse they just bought with your money. Oh! and don't forget, their face was freshly beat to the "gawds." Ha! Fabulous right? Absolutely Not!!! They are thieves.

We talked about some generational differences. But what exactly are the generation names and characteristics from our grand-parents lifespan down to ours.

I'm going to start with the generation from my dad's age, which is 78 on down to now. And why does it matter?

Each generation label serves as a short-hand to reference nearly 20 years of attitude, motivations, and historic events. Our attitudes, motivation, and historical events affect how we interact with others, what we believe is important and Fabulous, and values we instill in our offspring which ultimately has an effect on the future.

The Silent Generation. People were born in this generation between the mid-20's in the mid-40's (my dad was born in 1940). What was going on during that time frame?

According to Yolanda Williams course from study.com,[4] this generation refers to people who were born between 1925 and 1945. There are several theories as to where the label 'Silent Generation' originated. The children who grew up during this time worked very hard and kept quiet. It was commonly understood that children should be seen and not heard.

Sidebar: no wonder my dad treated us the way he did. I swear it was like don't speak to an adult unless you are being spoken to and dare not say "yes Sir" or "yes Ma'am" or you would get a whipping. My father started having kids late so most of my friend's parents are at least a decade younger than him, meaning they were born in the following generation.

Now back to the silent generation: During this time, the House Committee on Un-American Activities launched an assault on political freedom in America.

---

[4] https://study.com/academy/lesson/the-silent-generation-definition-characteristics-facts.html

This, in conjunction with Senator Joseph McCarthy's overzealous attempts to feed anti-communist sentiment in America, made it dangerous for people to speak freely about their opinions and beliefs. They became cautious about where they went and whom they were seen with. Therefore, the people were effectively 'silenced.'

In 1951, a *Time* magazine article was written in which the children of the generation were described as unimaginative, withdrawn, unadventurous, and cautious. *Time* magazine used the name 'Silent Generation' to refer to these individuals. The name has been used ever since. (I had to add this information or how else will we know why it was called the silent generation)

The Great Depression also happened during the Silent Generation. However, after 1939 when the depression ended those in the silent generation were able to take advantage of the new booming economy. Home mortgage rates were as low as 3%. Social Security and pensions were not under duress. And because of that most of them are currently financially secure in their old age and have been able to support their families greatly.

Baby Boomers were the next generation. Baby

boomers (also some were referred to as hippies) were born between the mid-40's and the mid-60's (My mother was born during this time). They are referred to as baby boomers due to the increase in birth rate after WWII. The postwar population increased incredibly and was described as a "boom" by newspapers and reporters. They grew up before smartphones and the internet ruled almost every aspect of our lives.

Here's what Del mar times commented: baby boomers make up a large portion of our economy, nearly 80 million.

The research that I did shows baby boomers could have had a large negative impact on our economy due to their reliance on government resources and less spending. However, now they are contributing greatly to the economy with the use of their resources, spending on healthcare, travel and assisted living.

Wikipedia says: baby boomers were the wealthiest, most active, and most physically fit generation up to the era in which they arrived and were amongst the first to grow up genuinely expecting the world to improve with time. They were also the generation that received peak levels of income; they could therefore reap the benefits of abundant levels of food, apparel and retirement programs.

My personal observation is that baby boomers are more settled in life due to their age. They are more established. They have real estate, financial savings and pensions.

Baby boomer women that I know, have recently gotten to know and just met through brief encounters are by far some of the most Fabulous women I've come in contact with.

Generation X the people in this generation were born between the mid-60's and the early to mid-80's (I was born during this time). According to Wikipedia, Generation Xers were children during a time of shifting societal values and were sometimes called the "latchkey generation". As a result of increasing divorce rates, increased maternal participation in the workforce, and prior to widespread availability of childcare options outside the home there was less adult supervision compared to previous generations. As adolescents and young adults, they were dubbed the "MTV Generation". Music videos were a big part of our lives. We watched a lot of TV because we were at home by ourselves often. Videos influenced the way we dressed and acted significantly. Even though we watched a lot of TV, we still valued listening to the radio, reading the newspaper and magazines thanks to our baby boomer parents.

We (Generation Xers) came up during the crack epidemic. This disproportionately impacted those of us living in urban areas because of drug turf wars and addiction. Even though most of the addicts were older than us, we got a firsthand view of the effects of drugs because at least one of our family members was a drug addict.

I remember my mom letting my uncle Tony stay with us for a while. We found drug needles around the house and in the couch. Thank goodness we never got stuck or even played with them. During that time in school and on the TV there was a big campaign to "Just Say No".

If that wasn't bad enough, AIDS emerged during the Generation X timeframe. AIDS was wiping people out! I saw this with my own eyes. My same uncle Tony died right before my eyes, when I was in the sixth grade, because of AIDS. He contracted it due to his drug use. My uncle Bobby died within the same year I believe, due to AIDS also. He was a homosexual. We, Gen Xers, were taught that sex could kill you.

Wikipedia noted: Guides regarding managing multiple generations in the workforce describe Gen Xers as: independent, resourceful, self-managing, adaptable, cynical, pragmatic, skeptical of authority, and as seeking a work life balance.

In a 2007 article published in the Harvard Business Review, demographers Strauss & Howe wrote of Generation X; "They are already the greatest entrepreneurial generation in U.S. history; their high-tech savvy and marketplace resilience have helped America prosper in the era of globalization."

I could go on and on about generation X just because I was born during that time and everything that was going on from then until now has greatly affected my ideals as well as motivated me to do the things that I'm doing today. I'm assuming I can make the same statement for all of us, whichever generation we were born in. Let's use what we've learned from our experiences to help the next generation, but we'll go into that later.

Now for the **Millennial's** (also known as Generation Y). They were born between the early to mid-80's until around 2004 (my daughter was born during this time). In positive ways, they are generally regarded as being more open-minded, and more supportive of equal rights for minorities. Other positives adjectives to describe them include confident, self-expressive, liberal, upbeat and receptive to new ideas and ways of living.

On the other hand, they've been described as lazy, narcissistic and prone to jump from job to job. The 2008 book "Trophy Kids" by Ron Alsop discusses how many young people have been rewarded for minimal accomplishments, such as mere participation, in competitive sports and have unrealistic expectations of working life.

A story in Time magazine said polls show that Millennials want flexible work schedules, more 'me time' on the job, and nearly nonstop feedback and career advice from managers. Another Time story in May 2013, titled "The Me Me Me Generation," begins: "They're narcissistic. They're lazy. They're coddled. They're even a bit delusional. Those aren't just unfounded negative stereotypes about 80 million Americans born roughly between 1980 and 2000. They're backed up by a decade of sociological research." The article also points out that Millennials may be simply adapting quickly to a world undergoing rapid technological change.

A 2012 study found Millennials to be "more civically and politically disengaged, more focused on materialistic values, and less concerned about helping the larger community than were Gen X and Baby Boomers at the same ages." According to USA Today, "The trend is more of an emphasis on extrinsic values such as money, fame, and image, and less emphasis on intrinsic values such as self-acceptance, group affiliation and community." The study was based on an analysis of two large databases of 9 million high school seniors and students entering college.

I found a lot of this to be true. Me just observing my daughter, nieces and nephews, all of who are millennials and their peers have confirmed many of the observations I just stated. Not only that, being in the business of beauty I've observed the conversations and behaviors of many millennials who have come to me for services.

The question is, what did I/we do to contribute to how millennial's interact in society today? We can't take the full blame because the social and political atmospheres at the time all of us were born affect us all. However, a large portion is what were we taught to value and what are we teaching our children to value now.

Example: If you value marriage, most likely your children will, and they will teach this to their children. Many today don't value marriage so many of our future offspring likely won't.

If you value higher education and instill it in your children, they are likely to do the same to their kids.

If you value the Bible and instill its teaching into your children, most likely your children will do the same with their children.

If you value and instill in your children the qualities of moral integrity and loyalty, they will most likely do the same to their children.

Now there won't be a 100% pass down rate but best believe the probability of passing meaningful qualities onto our children will be much higher than not.

This is the same if we pass along bad qualities. Example: if you are promiscuous and your children see multiple partners coming in and out of your bedroom then there is a greater probability that your children will do the same.

If you dropped out of school and you don't put a high value on education, if you do not instill the importance of your children attending school daily, there's a great probability that they won't value education.

If you could care less about religion or the Bible; you don't attend service or read the Bible; have your children attend service or read the Bible; if you don't talk about and could care less about anything that has to do with spirituality, then the probability is that your children will value godliness is slim to none.

If you are a liar and a cheat and your children observe this from you over the years as they grow up there's a great probability that they will portray the same qualities.

Where does that leave the future of our society? Now I'm going to pose this question again but not in the exact same way: What can I/we do to contribute to a better generation of people interacting in our society?

CHAPTER 4

WHAT'S THE PROBLEM NOW

The problem is, that for some of the reasons mentioned previously in this book, young women think that fabulousness consist of makeup, clothes, having a large derrière, the amount of followers they have on social media and all such similar things.

I'm going to expound on each statement I made and comment on what I believe many young people think Fabulousness is today. But before I do that let's think about all that we see around us today. Who are many of our misguided young one's role models today? When we turn on the TV and look at our phone and social media sites, what's the majority of what we see? Who creates the nation's standard of beauty? What music are we listening to? What impact does what we listen to have on our life? What TV shows or reality shows are getting the most ratings? How do the people we most admire look? How do they dress? Have you seen their lips go from nonexistent to prominent? Or their butts go from average to extremely large? Are we more concerned with those in the limelight than we are with securing our future and that of our family?

Young women relate make up to Fabulousness.

Young women now believe in always wearing makeup so much that they wear it constantly, even sleeping in it. Some don't want to be seen without foundation on. Many young ladies are altering their natural looks by drawing on new faces. They do this at the risk of their own skin.

I'm a makeup artist and I've seen the truth. I had a lovely young lady come into to my office one day. She was actually going to do some modeling for my accessory line. She was a talented dancer and seemed to have a beautiful personality. When she sat in my chair, I cleaned her face (as I do all of my clients before I start my work). Her face was riddled with dark pigmented acne scars, blemishes and bumps. She felt the need to tell me as I was removing her foundation that she couldn't seem to get rid of her acne. I gave her the best advice that I could. "Stop wearing the makeup" I said. "Stop wearing the makeup long enough for your skin to breathe and repair itself by using a good cleansing, toning, moisturizing and pigment repairing method." Although I'm a makeup artist, amongst other titles, I'm truly concerned with people. The moral code I live my life by will not allow me to mislead or deny good advice to someone just to secure my bag (income). My blessings will come in one form or another.

I knew that she would not take my advice even though she recognized it was in fact good. After all, as a young lady, who wants to be seen with bumps and blemishes all over their face. However, as long as she conceals them, will be as long as she will have them. Unfortunately, many of our young women are dealing with the same issue.

Makeup has been around for a very long time. Our methods of applying makeup have changed over time. The last several years, the makeup industry and those who wear it have grown tremendously.

It is my opinion that the current makeup application trends come heavily from the drag queen circuit. This is no offense to a drag queen or should I say, in many cases, a talented performer who happens to be a male impersonating a female. The point is, when a performer is applying makeup or having makeup applied to themselves, the composition tends to be heavier and dramatic. Due to the intense lighting that artist work under, the heavy makeup is required to accentuate their facial expressions. Under natural light this makeup looks cakey and overdone. Also, when a man is altering his look to become more feminine, he may add specific special touches with makeup to do so. This does not mean that every young woman learning to apply makeup should be using all of the same methods, especially on a daily basis. That's exactly what they're doing and that's why many young ladies' skin are suffering. Not to mention the fact that some are walking around looking overly dramatic as if they should be dancing across a stage with flashing lights upon them.

Of course, I had to take a little extra time on this topic because makeup happens to be one of my favorite subjects.

So, let's talk about how many young women feel that what they wear can make or break their Fabulosity. Of course, it is true most of us want to look nice when we step out. But is it just clothes, our outward appearance, that make us Fabulous?

Many young women would sit in my chair for

makeup either wearing or talking about what outfit they were going to wear. The sad truth is, in most cases, I knew when I saw them in the red bottoms and custom-made or name brand outfit, that they stole the money to get it. Now they may have not been knocking people over the head or robbing an actual bank, but anytime you use a credit card with a fake name on it, YOU ARE A THIEF. There have been countless young women in and out of my beauty bar fighting court cases for illegal activities all for the sake of looking good.

I mention this with all sincerity. It saddens me to see pretty, young, talented people making bad decisions that will surely affect their future derogatorily.

Many young women think that having a big butt makes them Fabulous.

Let me start by saying there's nothing wrong with wanting to have a nice shape. However, if this is all that you are fixated on, if you're willing to risk your life just to have it (outside of working out really hard), if you're willing to steal money or take what doesn't belong to you in order to pay for one (in other words, scheme the system), if paying for a booty job is more important than providing for your children, then sweetheart, honey, sugar, baby, dumpling you need to truly reevaluate your priorities.

There are countless TV, news and Internet stories of women who have risked their lives all in the name of getting a bigger behind. We've all seen them. You'd have to be living under a rock not to. Yet because of certain role models and new techniques this is still a much popular thing to do.

Love, get to know, understand you first. Then make any decision you want. It usually has the most satisfying results when you do it that way.

So now that you've got your make up on, you're dressed to the nine with your big booty protruding (of course), you've got to show your

Facebook, Instagram and Snapchat followers.

And you are definitely not relevant/Fabulous if you only have a few friends or followers, right? Unfortunately, this is what many of our young ones think.

These days, having a large social media following can be very instrumental in growing your business. But if you have no business and all you post is staged and fake and if the amount of likes you do or

don't receive for your pictures alter your mood, then
it may be time for you to reevaluate your priorities.

With the followers you achieve, will you be a
positive influencer? What is positivity in your eyes?

CHAPTER 5

(ROLE MODEL)
WHY I HAD TO SAY
SOMETHING

Role model

A role model is a person whose behavior, example,
or success is or can be emulated by others, especially
by younger people. The term "role model" is credited
to sociologist Robert K. Merton, who coined the
phrase during his career (Wikipedia).

It is my opinion that this world needs more positive
role models. The problem is we're coming up short
in the positive role model department because of
what many of our young ones or the newer
generation feel is fantastic, famed, fanciful and fine.
Instead, what is fabled, fake, false, fictitious and
fabricated is what is considered Fabulous.

Frank Sonnenberg wrote 13 ways to be a good role model in his book "Follow Your Conscious: Make a difference in your life and the lives of others".
What he wrote really hit the head on the nail. As he wrote about the things that a role model should and would do, he also wrote about the things they should not and would not do.

Here's his take (with a little of mine added to the end of each of his comments):

Hey big shot. You don't have to be a celebrity or a superstar to be a role model. Chances are if you're a parent, teacher, coach, religious leader, or manager, you're influencing people every day. Make it positive!

And if you consider yourself an Instagram celebrity, use your post and pictures wisely. You might just be able to help or inspire someone who's following you without even knowing it.

Set the bar high. Have high expectations for others *and* yourself. Avoid the tendency to adjust the target downward just to accommodate mediocrity.

This will keep you from making bad choices in

friends. This will lend to you being a good friend and/or companion. This will also keep you from expending too much time and energy on someone who doesn't deserve it.

Inspire others. When you're a role model, every message you send is critical. For example, people will notice whether or not you value a good education, the relationship that you have with your spouse, how you work under pressure, how you behave during the Little League game, and whether you're confident enough to admit fault. Don't wait for the stars to align to demonstrate good behavior. Deliver your message every day in small ways.

For this very reason I have always been skeptical of being filmed on a regular and in highly emotional situations. We all go through our periods when we are highly vulnerable or emotional. I'd hate to send the wrong signal or to damage my reputation by acting out on the big screen (although it could happen to the best of us).

Look in the mirror. Look to see if you're sending the wrong message. Here are some examples of behavior gone awry: cheating has become a substitute for hard work; you have become ruthless to get ahead; drugs are your rewards for success; life is about stuff, not people; relationships are disposable; the only thing that matters is winning.

When analyzing one's self, make sure if you see any of these bad qualities that you try to eradicate them immediately. Be truthful with yourself. Make sure you're not superficial. It's never too late to make positive changes.

Stand for something. Good role models are objective and fair. Furthermore, they have the strength of their convictions. They believe what they say and say what they believe. Mark Twain may have said it best, "Actions speak louder than words but not nearly as often."

Believe what you say. Say what you mean. Stand up for what's right even though it may not be popular.

Walk the talk. Ensure that your words and actions are consistent.

Back your words up with action as consistently as you can. This is the only way you can gain trust from those observing you (and believe me you are being watched if you are a role model).

Integrity matters. Good role models are open, honest, and trustworthy. Make sure to finish what you start and follow through on commitments.

According to Google definition: Integrity is the quality of being honest and having strong moral principles; moral uprightness.

Key synonyms that stand out to me are: honesty, honor, good character, principle(s), ethics, morals, righteousness, morality, virtue, deceny, fairness, scru pulousness, sincerity,
truthfulness and trustworthiness.

Vocabulary.com put it well when it said having integrity means doing the right thing in a reliable way. It's a personality trait that we admire, since it means a person has a moral compass that doesn't waver. It literally means having "wholeness" of character.

I think it's so important that people understand what integrity really means. Being a person of integrity is genuinely Fabulous. I pride myself after always striving for moral integrity. In the world we live in, maintaining this quality can be a true challenge. Young role models, understand this words true meaning now please. Reflect on its description often.

Be respectful. Treat others as you want to be treated.

Always stay humble. True, you may be elevated in finance, education or class over someone else. Do not let that go to your head. Let's not forget what Maya Angelou once wrote, "We are more alike, my friends, than we are unalike."

Despite any differences, here are five ways we all are alike according to Eric Torrence's article [5], I'm sharing this because I find it to be undeniable truth.

1. **We all have a story**

People aren't statistics, though we often treat each other that way. We have a story – and if we give each other the opportunity, we actually like to tell it. We all came from somewhere, and we've all experienced challenges, struggles, and victories that have shaped us into who we are and what we believe.

Asking someone to tell you his or her story will almost always lead to common ground. Hearing

---

[5] https://www.thindifference.com/2017/07/5-ways-we-are-all-alike/

someone else's story helps me put myself in their shoes. It makes me appreciate that this person is a person, not a statistic. And, it reminds me that they are on a journey, just like me.

2. **We all are afraid**

Whether we would admit it or not, we are all afraid of something. To us, our fears seem perfectly rational, even when others might find them strange. As we get to know people's stories, perhaps we'll discover our fears aren't all that different. And, even if someone is afraid of something we aren't, maybe we can at least find common ground around the crippling power of fear and wrestle together with how to overcome it together.

3. **We all are stuck in our own skin**

Which means we are limited by our own perspective. You can't fully understand me because you haven't walked in my shoes. And, I can't fully understand you, because I haven't lived in your skin.
But, doesn't this actually unite us a bit? Every person you meet is limited. And, every person needs help to see a bigger perspective. No one has all the answers or sees everything clearly. Finding common ground often starts with recognizing our limitations;

and since we're all limited, we're in good company.

4. **We all are valuable**

Every person is worthy of respect. I believe God has gifted every person with creativity, responsibility, and dignity. Whether you agree, dignity is bestowed on us by God (or whether you believe in God at all), you probably believe people are incredibly valuable. We all cringe when someone is treated as "less than," or when their dignity is taken from them by someone else. Whenever people are turned into objects for pleasure or control, something within us should be outraged – because we inherently know people shouldn't be treated that way. It's why abuse, sexism, racism, racial inequality, slavery, neglect, and many other human and civil rights issues are abhorrent.

Finding common ground starts with remembering the person we are talking to has inherent value. Recognizing this value should change the way we approach a person with whom we disagree. It should lead us to civility.

5. **We all are imperfect**

Another common phrase we all say is, "I'm not perfect." And the truth is, you aren't. And neither am I.

Most of the time, we are incredibly forgiving of ourselves for our imperfections; however, we also tend to be incredibly forgetful that others are just as imperfect as we are. We give ourselves loads of grace for making a hasty comment, a rude interjection, or angry response. But if someone does that to us, watch out!

Finding common ground means giving the same grace we give ourselves to others. It means recognizing we will make mistakes, and others will make mistakes with us.

Remembering these things will help us to treat others with respect. This does not mean it will be easy, sometimes it can be downright hard. Keep in mind you can always respectfully agree to disagree. And even if you choose not to deal with a person or a situation you can handle it or them with dignity and respect.

Believe in yourself. Be confident in who you are and what you represent. But balance that confidence with a dose of humility.

I spoke of humility. Make sure you add confidence to it. Some people feel they can't be confident and humble. That is totally not true. Always remember there is a difference between arrogance and confidence. You cannot be an influencer without confidence. Confidence is an important quality to have in order to be fabulous.

Hold people accountable. Don't accept bad behavior. Speak up against abuses. If you don't condemn poor behavior, then you're a co-conspirator. Life isn't a spectator sport.

This is so true. When you do not speak out about bad behavior it's just like you taking part in it. I'm not talking about the things that you see on TV. I'm talking about things that are up close and personal. Those things that you witness right in front of your face or in your vicinity. Reasonably do what you can to make a difference?

Accept responsibility for your actions. When you make a mistake, admit fault and show you mean it by taking corrective action.

It is okay and quite acceptable to apologize if you've made a mistake or offended someone.
Let me make this clear. This does not mean that if

you say something or do something in line with your moral compass or integrity that offends someone else, you must apologize for what you said or did. You can, however try your best to keep peace while remaining true to your moral standard. It is okay to agree to disagree. And you can like someone personally but not agree with or like an action that they take.

On the other hand, because of our imperfection, we will make mistakes. We may do or say something that we should absolutely say sorry for. Owning up to our mistakes and making corrections when needed is a sign of strength, not weakness.

You are judged by the company you keep. Surround yourself with people of high character and integrity. They may rub off on you and provide extra encouragement when the stakes are high or the going gets tough.

Quite simple, role models have role models.

Your soul is **NOT** for sale. Listen to your conscience. That's why you have one.

Most of us have been asked the question: Would you

do it for a million dollars? Do what? Anything that you normally wouldn't do or that your conscience wouldn't under any other circumstances allow you to do. Would you do it for the money? Stay true to yourself.

With that being said...

My daughter was 17 years old when I started writing this book. She turned 18 as I was finishing it. I am concerned about her and every other young (this includes souls in their 20's and 30's) person who could possibly be allowing this world's trend to influence what they feel about themselves and how Fabulous they are. These young people will play a tremendously large role in shaping the future of our society.

How I relate...

I left home at the age of 17. I got married at the age of 20 for all the wrong reasons. After finding out my mother was terminally ill and determined to move from Chicago to Georgia, I was trying to find security in the wrong place for the wrong reasons. By the age of 21 my mother had passed away from cancer. I played a major role in taking care of her before she died. It was a traumatizing experience. I watched my mother's flesh rot away. I was lost afterwards.

Although I was married, I had no security or support. I had isolated myself from 2 of the closest people who were in my corner when I left home originally. It seemed like my world was falling apart. By the age of 22, not only had I lost a child but my marriage fell apart (again might I add). With me struggling to piece together a marriage that I should have let fall apart completely, I got pregnant again with my estranged husband's child. At the age of 23 I found myself in the hospital on bed rest before giving birth to my 1.4 pound daughter.

During the days and months in between the timeline of my life mentioned here, I made decisions based on what I felt about myself as a person. I didn't realize at the time that I was making decisions based on my own definition of Fabulosity. With all that was going on around me I was unfocused. I hit so many potholes that I wish I could've avoided. Some of the effects, good and bad, have lasted to this very day.

At the time I thought (heck I knew), I was fine as wine. When I walked out the house my hair was laid and I had my best on. I could go from the house to work to the club with what I put on every morning. I even dressed like I was going to a cocktail reception just to walk to the corner store. But I did not understand my worth nor did I know myself enough at the time. You couldn't tell me that back then. I lived the next decade or more through trial, tribulation and error.

Not having my mother to turn to for support and advice when things seemed to be falling apart was at times depressing and sobering. Not having a present or supportive father or husband made things very difficult at times also. But dealing with my lot in life also made me stronger. The good business character my mother instilled in me during my younger teenage years helped me to go on as an entrepreneur when things got rough.

During my daughter's three month plus stent in the hospital, she/we (she and I) overcame a stage 2 brain bleed, a heart murmur surgery, and surgery on her eyes due to retinopathy of prematurity. It wasn't until after she came home from the hospital that my husband/her father and I got back together. I started selling accessories on the weekends from salon to salon in the Chicago land area. I stopped working during the week to stay with our daughter because she was still very small when she came home (a little over 4 pounds) and was at risk of catching RSV (a respiratory virus that can easily take a premature infant's life).We were together for less than a year when he left and took all the money we had.

What do you think I did next? After crying my eyes out, I sobered up and went into full hustle mode. I worked harder to meet new people and sold my fashion accessories all over the city of Chicago. I got back to doing makeup. I made it my business to look my best even though I was working through one of the hardest times in my life. Looking good myself and helping others to do the same made me feel much better. I even started making fur ponchos and sold them all over the city. My company eventually came to be known as Accessory Me and its motto is "Look Good, Feel Good, Be Successful".

Even though at the time I was a one-woman show, I referred to my business as my company. It was my dream to grow and expand and over time. By not letting go of my aspirations, I began to see the fruit of my labors while climbing my own ladder of success.

I share this because as I reflect on my life situations and choices, I can't help but to think, this could be my daughter, or my cousin's daughter or my niece and some other sincere young person's encounter in life. I went through the trials and tribulations to add some direction and pothole warnings on the map to Fabulosity.

I did not have the support and direction of my family while going through some of my most difficult hardships but I can try to lend a helping hand through words of and advice because of the knowledge and wisdom that I've gained through the years while overcoming my hurdles. I can be in influencer and a role model. And so can my daughter. And so can you!
This is why I had to say something.

CHAPTER 6

MAYBE WE CAN HELP (EACH ONE TEACH ONE)

Let me start this chapter off by saying, I know we can help. I used the word maybe because any helpful words or direction given will only work if you take heed and allow them to.

Now, who is we? Of course, it's the **Fabulous 40 & Over Club**. Which consist of those of us who have navigated through some parts of life that you (younger people) haven't been through yet or are going through right now. Those of us who have learned from the mistakes that we've made, some of which you may be about to make and could possibly avoid. These experiences have shaped our view of life, truth, and our definition of true Fabulousness.

I am from Chicago and any and everyone who knows about Chicago knows that because of the extreme weather and the salt treatments to the streets, there are many potholes. These holes, if driven across too fast, heck sometimes even slowly, can potentially wreck your car or cause tremendous damage that is very expensive to repair. Because I've been navigating around the city for so long, I know how to avoid many of the potholes, especially those in the area of my home and business. If you were new to the city would you not appreciate a road map that shows you how to avoid those crippling potholes? Anyone in their right mind would say yes.

I hope that using that illustration can help one to see and appreciate the reason why a mature point of view can be of assistance. We have already hit some of life's potholes. We've paid many costs for life repairs. We have grown immune to some of life's viruses/problems.

What I'm attempting to accomplish now, with the help of others, is to draw a map highlighting some of life's dangerous potholes that play a part in shaping a negative view of ourselves, give us a false sense of Fabulousness, and that the veer us off the course of positivity.

Here are several major potholes you'll need to avoid. Drugs, baby daddies and/or mama's (you see how I used the plural form of those words), domestic/physical abuse, low self-esteem and depression. These are a few, however, they are major obstacles that can affect our lives negatively and sometimes permanently if will allow them.

Let's analyze each one of these points briefly.

Drugs:
According to Better Health: Different types of drugs affect your body in different ways, and the effects associated with drugs can vary from person to person. How a drug effects an individual is dependent on a variety of factors including body size, general health, the amount and strength of the drug, and whether any other drugs are in the person's system at the same time. It is important to remember that illegal drugs are not controlled substances, and therefore the quality and strength may differ from one batch to another.

Drugs can have short-term and long-term effects. These effects can be physical and psychological and can include dependency.

You may act differently, feel differently and think differently if you have taken drugs. And you may struggle to control your actions and thoughts.

Let's stop right there. A year and a half ago I put my six-year-old son in the car so that I could run some errands. There was some commotion on the block we lived. I didn't quite know what was going on, however as I was approaching the end of the block, I saw a young man, who had stripped himself butt naked. He was having some sort of a fit in the middle of the street. I'd seen this young man walking in the neighborhood several times before. The ambulance had to come get him. Not only was I worried about him, I was worried about the impression that left on my son...

I also know of young lady who doesn't have her full faculties because of drugs that she took previously. Sometimes you can take the wrong thing and it alters your mind permanently.

The thing is, much of the rap music and songs today glorify the use of drugs. It seems all too crazy, in my opinion. Some impressionable minds are being caught up in the hype. Killing your brain cells over time is certainly not Fabulous. Beware.

Baby daddies:
Here's some things Babygaga had to say in an article written by Liegh_Hewet that talked about confessions from 15 women with multiple baby

daddies. Here are a few of them and what Liegh had to say about it.

Often times, these moms have a stigma that follows them throughout their lives that they are easy or used goods. Many of these ladies admit that it's not easy and each share their own personal struggles. From feeling like they'll never date again to being fed up with all the judgment that can be sent their way. These women are not holding back. Others put on a brave face and stand up for themselves, owning up to their mistakes and demanding respect.

For the most part, many of these moms have deep regrets. Sometimes, they hate that they have different kids with different men. They might feel embarrassed or ashamed about their situation. Often times, these ladies feel heartache that their life did not turn out as they expected and mourn the loss of the chance to have a happy family.

One young woman she wrote about has 3 children with 3 different men and admits that she's pretty ashamed of her situation. One father lives in a different state, so he isn't in their child's life. The second father is serving time in prison for 20 years, so he's obviously out. Finally, we have the 3rd father who is around and spends time with their kid. Thank goodness that at least one man is stepping up and taking responsibility for his actions.

This couldn't be an easy situation to be in and I can see why she might be ashamed of the choices she's made in men over the years. Between the absent dad and the one that's incarcerated, it's clear that she didn't have the best judgment in men. At least the 3rd dad is around but that's not much of a consolation prize for the other children.

She wrote about another young lady. This confessor wants to know if it's bad that she's only 20-years-old and is pregnant with her third child. Not only that, but each of her kids has a different dad. She defends herself, claiming she was in love with each man at the time that she became pregnant. This girl must fall in love at the drop of a hat. It's heartbreaking that she believes in love so much that she can't seem to learn her lesson.

I hope for her sake, and the sake of her children, that she takes some time to slow down and deal with her self-esteem issues before moving on to the next man. I don't mean to be judgy but maybe as she matures a bit, she'll realize what a treasure she is and what a gift her children are. It can't be easy to be that young and be a single mom.

Another confessor admits that she has a 7-month-old baby and is pregnant again but by a different dad.

This is revealing enough but I think that it is the last admission that gives us the most insight into how immature this girl really is. The fact that she is scared to be made fun of shows just how out-of-whack her priorities are.

I get it, though. What she really means is that she is afraid that she will be judged for having two kids with two different dads. I feel for young girls who find themselves in this difficult situation and hope for her sake that she ends up getting the support that she needs. Hopefully, no one will actually make fun of her for the fact that she made some questionable choices. Everybody makes mistakes and she deserves happiness.

One confessor has two kids with two different dads and really doesn't care what you think about it. As a matter of fact, she covers just about every judgment she's probably ever experienced and rips each one to shreds. First of all, having multiple dads doesn't mean that she's easy. This mom admits to making mistakes when she was younger and owns up to the fact that she can't change the choices that she made. Also, she would like everyone to know that she's not the same as she once was and claims that she has totally grown up. So, go ahead and forget about judging this woman or giving her any grief for having multiple daddies for her kids. If everyone took on this attitude, then the world would be a much better place.

I agree with what the last confessor shared here. Who are we to judge and many of us make mistakes that we learn from? At the same time, wouldn't it be better if we could just avoid some of these mistakes. For those who don't have kids yet, take heed to what you read. If you only have one child and you and the child's father are no longer together, before you have another one, take heed to what you read. It's you and your child's life. What do you want for your family?

Domestic/Physical abuse:
is also referred to as domestic violence, intimate partner violence (IPV), and relationship abuse. According to womenshealth.gov: violence against women can cause long-term physical and mental health problems. Violence and abuse affect not just the women involved but also their children, families, and communities. These effects include harm to an individual's health, possibly long-term harm to children, and harm to communities such as lost work and homelessness.
 The article states: short-term physical effects of violence can include minor injuries or serious conditions. They can include bruises, cuts, broken

bones, or injuries to organs and other parts inside of your body. Some physical injuries are difficult or impossible to see without scans, x-rays, or other tests done by a doctor or nurse.

Short-term physical effects of sexual violence can include:

Vaginal bleeding or pelvic pain
Unwanted pregnancy
Sexually transmitted infections (STI's), including HIV (that's a long-term affect in my opinion)
Trouble sleeping or nightmares
If you are pregnant, a physical injury can hurt you and the unborn child. This is also true in some cases of sexual assault.

If you are sexually assaulted by the person you live with, and you have children in the home, think about your children's safety also. Violence in the home often includes child abuse. Many children who witness violence in the home are also victims of physical abuse.

Violence against women, including sexual or physical violence, is linked to many long-term health problems.
These can include:

Arthritis

Asthma

Chronic pain

Digestive problems such as stomach ulcers

Heart problems

Irritable bowel syndrome

Nightmares and problems sleeping

Migraine headaches

Sexual problems such as pain during sex

Stress

Problems with the immune system

Many women also have mental health problems after violence.

To cope with the effects of the violence, some women start misusing alcohol or drugs or engage in risky behaviors, such as having unprotected sex. Sexual violence can also affect someone's perception of their own body, leading to unhealthy eating patterns or eating disorders.

I personally want to stress the fact that domestic abuse is and can be more than physical. Just because your spouse does not outright hit you or hurt you physically does not mean you're not a victim of abuse. If you are getting multiple STI's from your partner, they are abusing you (we will address why it is that people allow themselves to be abused in non-physical forms). If your partner is tearing you down verbally, you are being abused. If your partner is being mentally controlling, giving you the silent treatment or withholding acts of love any time you act in a manner that they don't approve and for very small reasons (to the point that you have anxiety anytime you deal with them), you are a victim of abuse.

Mental abuse can lead to our next and last major potholed mentioned in this chapter.

Low self-esteem which can lead to **Depression**. An article on psych alive.org by Lena Firestone speaks of low self-esteem:

Low self-esteem is characterized by a lack of confidence and feeling badly about oneself. People with low self-esteem often feel unlovable, awkward, or incompetent. According to researchers Morris Rosenberg and Timothy J. Owens, who wrote Low Self-esteem People: A Collective Portrait, people with low self-esteem tend to be hypersensitive. They have a fragile sense of self that can easily be wounded by others.

Furthermore, people with low self-esteem are *"hypervigilant and hyperalert to signs of rejection, inadequacy, and rebuff,"* writes Rosenberg and Owens. Often, individuals lacking self-esteem see rejection and disapproval even when there isn't any. "The danger always lurks that [they] will make a mistake, use poor judgement, do something embarrassing, expose [themselves] to ridicule, behave immorally or contemptibly. Life, in all its variety, poses an ongoing threat to self-esteem."

A few sources of low self-esteem are

Disapproving authority figures:

When someone of authority in your life such as your parent or teacher makes you feel as if nothing you do is right; If you are criticized constantly no matter how hard you try, it can cause you to feel like a failure and affect your self-esteem.

Uninvolved/preoccupied parents or caregivers:

If your parents or primary caregivers don't pay attention to any of your achievements, if they go on as if they don't notice anything you do, it can result in you feeling unimportant.

Bullying:

We know what bullying is. But what we may not understand is that grown people can be bullied too. Bullying can cause a person to feel   unsafe and unsure of him or herself.

Trauma:

Physical, sexual and/or emotional abuse can cause low self-esteem. If forced into a physical sexual or emotional position against your will, it can be very hard to like the world or trust yourself and others. It could even cause you to blame yourself for situations that you had no control over.

Society and the Media:
 Many of the people we see in the media and magazines are packed and airbrushed into unrealistic levels of beauty. Many of them have had surgeries and procedures that we can't even afford. It's an epidemic that's getting worse as each day passes. It can make a person feel as if they are inadequate. It is unfair to compare yourself to almost intangible, fictitious, fraudulent, and fabled beauty. That truly does not define Fabulousness.

Any or all of these potholes can cause us to become depressed.

Depression:
Causes severe symptoms that affect how you feel, think, and handle daily activities, such as sleeping, eating, or working. Severe depression can even cause you to have suicidal thoughts.

Watch out for yourselves! Remember that each of us are valuable, we are unique yet similar (none of us is inherently better than the other), and as long as we have freedom, life, breath and health we have the potential to achieve our dreams.

Listen and take heed to the stories we share in the next couple of chapters. These are words of Inspiration, Motivation andTruth, shared by myself and others who are concerned about you. I said it. We may not know you personally but that does not mean we don't care. We have daughters and sons, nieces and nephews, grandchildren and godchildren and even younger friends dealing with some of the same things you are. And as I said earlier, I'm pretty sure many of us have gone through, if not exactly what you're dealing with, definitely something similar. My hopes are that you learn from some of our mistakes before you have to make them yourself and/or you find the Encouragement and Motivation you need to get through whatever it is you're dealing with while knowing it's possible because we've done it ourselves.

(If you are having a hard time dealing with any of the things mentioned in this chapter don't be afraid to seek professional help.)

This is your Fabulosity Compass. It's a valuable tool that's going help navigate or guide you through some serious obstacles in life. Learn how to use it wisely as you journey to Fabulosity.

CHAPTER 7

SHARING IS CARING
A PIECE OF ME

As if I haven't already shared many pieces of me, right? Ha!

Well, the next two chapters of this book consist of a questionnaire compiled by me. I've asked every Fabulous 40 and over woman to answer each of the questions and share something about themselves along with any words of Inspiration, Motivation and Encouragement for all of you readers. So, I will start with myself. Let's get even more personal.

Name:

My name is Miki Riley. Or should I say I'm most commonly known as Miki Riley. I was married to my daughter's father, whose last name is Riley, over 20 years ago. I kept the name even after our divorce because I did not want my daughter's name to be identified as different from my own. After going into business for myself, with my accessory and real estate appraisal company, I became most popularly known as Miki Riley. So, in the past, due to business, thus my name.

I most recently like to be identified as just Miki.

I am currently married (have been as of the past eight years) and my husband's last name is Rolling. I will most likely be changing my legal name to match.

Now, wasn't that the longest answer you've gotten for the question "what is your name?"

I told you in this chapter's title I was going to give you a piece of me ;-)

Age: 41

Occupation: Serial entrepreneur, licensed insurance agent, semi-truck owner with a CDL license and small transport company, makeup artist/instructor, accessory consultant/distributor, owner/founder of Accessory Me, The Fabulous 40 & Over Club, The FAB (Fierce And Beautiful) Project NFP, and most recently- Author.

How do I define the word Fabulous:

Being fabulous is much more than outer attractiveness. It's outstanding qualities that are the main ingredient to Fabulousness. Confidence due to self-worth, Accomplishment due to hard work, Compassion due to humility, modesty, and the love of goodness. And Generosity due to the same. In my opinion, these are the most important words to define Fabulousness. Add those things, first, to a fashion forward (and tasteful) wardrobe, hair and naturally glammed face and Boom! FABULOUS!!!

What I feel my greatest accomplishment is thus far:

I forgot to add, outside of whatever you feel you've accomplished spiritually because of your relationship with God. Why? Because I feel that should always trump anything else. So, to answer that question, I'd have to say, writing this book and making sure that it is presentation worthy so far has been my greatest accomplishment currently. I've learned so much just doing research on topics outlined in this book. It helped me learn about and understand my daughter even more. It helped me understand more about the past, present and possible future. It helped me want to extend myself more. It has motivated me to do and be even better for myself and for anyone I can have an impact on.

What challenges did I face while working toward my accomplishment:

I spoke this book into existence a little over a year

ago. It's title never changed from the inception. I knew also that this would be an actual club one day. I began to try to get people involved and excited to give back in a way that would be encouraging. I offered free lunches just to get people out to discuss what I was trying to do. I would say my biggest challenge has been to get mature women REALLY involved and not just saying that this sounds like a wonderful idea and that they are on board but actuality not showing up or finding the time to participate. Posting up encouraging words and sometimes barely even getting a few comments was hard sometimes also. But I've still been determined. And if you read this and you haven't gotten as involved as you could, there's always a place for your participation and inspiration. I know that many of us have a lot on their plates but if you can make room for just a little more, do so with the Fabulous 40 & Over Club when you can.

Is there anything I hope to accomplish in the near future:
My goal is to have at least 1000 active Fabulous 40 & Over Club members by this time next year.

Are there any challenges that I'm currently facing to reach my most current goal that I'd like to share: I would have to say just staying focused and relentless until I reach my goal. Making sure the right people on my team who also would like to see the Fabulous 40 and Over Club grow and not wasting my resources in the wrong directions, I would say has been my most recent challenge.

A short story I'd like to share while on my journey to Fabulousness:
(as if I haven't shared enough) I'm going to keep this brief because I have shared a lot about me already. Here's something about me that I did not discuss. I've been dealing with depression since I was a young teenager. I don't know if it was because of my strained relationship with my mother or maybe just a chemical imbalance. I'd sleep extremely long hours in hopes the time would just pass me by.
Experiences I had in life were at times emotionally crippling. But somehow my losses gave me great strength to go on. I could only lie down so long before I had to get up and make life happen. After all, my children are relying on me. And knowing that makes me get up anyway on those days when I feel I can barely make it. It makes me work through my anxiety and push on through to my goals.

Words of Inspiration or Encouragement:
this is going to sound so simple but, if I can do it so can you. You have the full potential to be who and

what you want to be despite your circumstances, past or present. Even if you have made mistakes, as we all have, you can realize your goals. If you have given up on making goals, you can start again today and every day you are alive!

CHAPTER 8

39 OTHER STORIES TO INSPIRE

Name: Twanda Scott

Age: 46

Occupation: Underwriter Technician

How do you define Fabulous: It depends on what vantage point you look at when it comes to Fabulousness? You know I could be Fabulous today because I may be feeling myself, but I know that I've accomplished something that I've set forth to do. That's Fabulousness in a nutshell to me. Accomplishment, and feeling yourself.

What do you consider your greatest accomplishment is thus far: For me, it has been to move to a state where I had no family support as a single parent, to accomplish buying a house, setting my family up in and maintaining without the support of a spouse and family locally to catch me if I should fall.

Challenges while working towards your accomplishment: This taught me the importance of learning myself as well as learning how to be strong when I feel weak and vulnerable. But also built character that allowed me to withstand the trials of doing it alone when I always thought that I needed someone beside me.

Anything you look forward accomplishing in the near future:
My 5 to 10 your goal is to be completely debt-free and pay off my home. That's physically, now spiritually I would like to explore serving in other countries in my ministry and to continue to grow in my love for my heavenly father Jehovah.

Story while on your journey to Fabulousness: I had to battle with my child's fathers over custody. I've had to overcome financial ruin and I've struggled with believing in myself. Yet I've been able to rise above these things and to reach my greatest accomplishments thus far

Words of inspiration/encouragement: Never give up on yourself! It's okay to doubt, but you have to believe that your purpose is not the struggle but where you are going.

Name: Kara Robinson Smith

Age: 56

How do you define the word Fabulous: A person that is real sure of themselves. To feel really good about yourself to me is Fabulous, to be sure, to be confident, to be able to not be worried about what someone else thinks. You knowing you, just being you, good health is Fabulous.

What do you consider your greatest accomplishment is thus far: Being able to raise my four children and seeing the results of that which are my grandchildren.

What challenges did you face while working toward your goal: Health issues those are my biggest challenges and serving my God. I was diagnosed with cervical cancer years ago. I was told it was stage IV. However, after laser surgery my cancer was gone thank goodness, thank my God.

Is there anything that you hope to accomplish in the near future: I want to move to Dubai.

Are there any challenges that you are currently facing to reach your current goal: Yes I'm dealing with the same issues as before, health. As the old saying goes, "the body is the temple," so that is my greatest issue. I currently have fibromyalgia, diabetes and other issues. My most important goal is to take care of me.

A short story you'd like to share while on your journey to Fabulousness: I've been married three times. And within those different marriages, (there was Donald there was Donnie who was the father of my 2 children and there was another one that I don't even feel like naming) In each one of my marriages, I have truly learned how to, as they say, "live and survive." They each gave me something. Without the lessons whether they are good or bad, each one of them taught me something that helped me live and survive.

Words of inspiration/encouragement: Being a black female, whatever your goals are, do whatever is necessary to reach them. Not only reaching but completing them.

Name: Bonnie Jones

Age: 67

Occupation: Administrative Assistant

How do you define Fabulous: Confident, optimistic and spiritual.

What do you consider your greatest accomplishment thus far: Being a mentor for young people.

What challenges did you face while working toward your goal: Trying to be a good listener and having empathy for others. Also, trying to understand others circumstance and having patience.

Is there anything you hope to accomplish in the near future: I want to always be a source of encouragement to others. That's what I'd like to accomplish. I'd like to leave this earth knowing that I've had a positive influence on someone.

Any challenges you may be facing while working toward this: Keeping my mouth shut. Knowing when to speak and when not to speak. And not being so opinionated.

A short story you'd like to share while on your journey to Fabulousness: I was in a situation where I had to mentor a young person who would quit high school. I had to learn to be understanding, patient, considerate and firm. This young lady now is doing well. She got back into school and graduated from high school. She now has an Associate's degree. She found out that she loves school, she's much more outgoing now and she has more confidence in herself. To know I played a part in this brings me great joy and a sense of accomplishment.

Words of inspiration/encouragement: Be true to yourself. Believe in yourself. Set boundaries of behavior on how you want to be treated.

Name: Catherine Roberson

Age: 51

Occupation: Housewife

Definition of Fabulous: Compassionate, empathetic, loving and forgiving. Being forgiving is Fabulous.

What would you consider your greatest accomplishment is thus far: Outside of solidifying my relationship with Jehovah, I would say marrying my best friend is my greatest accomplishment.

Challenges while working toward your accomplishment: Being unsure of myself and being insecure led to jealousy. I was able to overcome, my insecurity as I grew older and learned that Life works itself out

Near future Goals: Every day is an adventure for me. My husband has given me the marriage of my dream. I have great friends. And I'm confident that whatever life has in store I will succeed and overcome any challenge.

A short story you'd like to share while on your journey to Fabulousness: One thing I've learned is everyone needs a confidant and don't ever betray their trust. Keep your friends secrets close to your heart. I have friends that tell me so many things and many times I'm just their listening ear.

Words of inspiration/encouragement: Life is not fair but it's still good. I love that quote. I don't remember where I will read it but I found it to be so true..

Name: Leslie Cooper

Age: 44

Occupation: P. A

How do you define Fabulous: A person who gets out there and gets it, a provider. It's not always about outer beauty, it's about how you feel inside, your daily attitude about life and being true to yourself makes you Fabulous.

Greatest accomplishment thus far: Getting my DCFS license for Foster children

Challenges while working towards your accomplishment: Getting sick due to having lupus and still having to attend class.

Future Accomplishments: Opening up my day care

Current Challenges: No challenges. I just stay focused on my life plans and don't let anything get in the way of me achieving them

Short Story: I have experienced my worst nightmare. I always knew since a long time ago thought I might lose my eyesight. At an early age I was diagnosed with genetic eye disease. I found out at the age of 38 I have lupus. Within two years of me finding out about my illness I was sitting in my kitchen watching TV and noticed that I couldn't see out of my right eye. I got nervous and scared. I called my friend and told her I can't see and needed to go to the hospital. I cried. I think my friend cried too. We both were scared. My friend Miki was right there asking all the questions. The hospital couldn't do anything for me and told me that my eyes were healthy. The doctors didn't know what was happening. I was told to follow up with my specialist, so I did just that. I went to the Illinois Eye Intuition. They specialize in eye care. They ran several tests to see what was going on. The doctor told me that I had a blood clot in my eye. It was blocking my vision and they needed to drain the blood off my eye every week until it cleared up so I can regain some of my sight back. I then went home and cried, called my sister and cried even more. Miki and my sister Tonie were there every step of the way, taking me to the clinic every Friday morning to get the injection in my eye, cheering me on saying, "you can do it, you're a big girl." The pain that I experienced was the worst! Having a needled inserted in my eye every weekend and still going to work afterwards was extremely hard. Still, not one time did I complain. People would say "why are you at work?" I said I have kids to take care of and a house to run, no time to take off. Months went by, the same thing every Friday my sister would take me to the clinic for the same procedure. I can say my sister and friend kept me uplifted along with my children. I'm so grateful for the support system that I have. One day I woke up and said, "I can see, I can see!" I called my sister, Miki and daughter and shared the good news. I'm so grateful for my doctor and the staff at U. I. C. for a job well done. Now I'm living my life to the fullest. Giving up wasn't in the plan. I'm a fighter so let me keep fighting. Lupus will not kill me or take anything from me without a fight.

Words of inspiration/encouragement: My words of inspiration are, don't give up on what you want in life. Be true to yourself. Love who you were and who you have become. Be the best at whatever you desire. Don't let illness, relationships or anything get in your way of reaching your goals and you are never too young or too old to have a goal.

Name: LaVonna Jackson

Age: 50

Occupation: Mental Health Therapist

How do you define Fabulous: I feel like being Fabulous is accepting myself for not only my good but also my bad qualities. It's growth, it's about knowing that you don't have to be perfect. You are perfect if you have a relationship with God, if you strive to do the right things, if you have appropriate levels of self-esteem and know that you are worthy to be treated with love and respect.

Greatest Accomplishment: Although I have completed many personal accomplishments, including earning three Degrees, having a thriving career, traveling the world and raising two beautifully accomplished daughters, I define my success through my relationship with myself, my loved ones and most importantly with God.

Challenges: After two decades of marriage to my teenage sweetheart, I suddenly became a young widow and a single parent of two teenage daughters. Feeling lost and alone, I was forced into a new way of life, a new way of thinking and the challenge of taping into strength that I never knew I had.

Future Accomplishments: I am currently working on a book about Grief, I plan to do more public speaking and of course more traveling. The world is a big place and I never get tired of exploring it!

Current Challenges: I would love to remarry again. I've found relationships to be challenging in the times that we're currently living in. Dating has changed, values have changed and quite frankly expectations have been lowered. I am still hopeful however that someday God will send me another SOULMATE to share on the journey of life.

Short Story: The most important lesson that I've learned on this journey is that I am the GATEKEEPER to my Fabulousness. Fabulousness can be terribly flawed by allowing the wrong influences in your presence or your psyche. Fabulousness is a state of mind, a state of self-love.

Words of inspiration/encouragement: In order for things to work out favorable, you must believe that it will!

Name: Melody Smith

Age: 40

Fabulous Definition: The confidence within you

Occupation: Probation Officer, CEO of Drops of Chocolate Ent. Model Academy, Lushious Lush Lingerie consultant, booking manager for Accessory Me Beauty Bar, Insurance Agent, and Entrepreneur

Greatest Accomplishment: My greatest accomplishment is balancing my life. As the Founder/CEO of Drops of Chocolate Entertainment, I embarked on a vision to start Drops of Chocolate Plus Size Modeling Academy. It is a model training and development program exclusively for plus size women. Established in 2015, we provide training and guidance. We also help launch the careers of plus size models, many of who will appear in print ads, runway showcases, television programs, online magazines, designer showcases, pageants and much more. We also offer a variety of personal development and lifestyle workshops for the plus-size woman. I myself am a plus model who now specializes in plus size model training, development, and management. I'm an advocate and supporter of increasing the visibility of fuller figures on fashion runways. In 2009, I successfully started Drops of Chocolate Entertainment as a networking, event planning and promoting company. I added this entity to the company in 2015 as a modeling development academy. Drops of Chocolate Plus Size Modeling Academy is one of Chicago's first training programs exclusively for aspiring plus size models. I am always willing to share my gift of inspiring other women with self-esteem, fitness, career, educational and life goals. I decided to embark on a vision from God. I have a passion about this industry and have researched many different topics regarding body image, plus size modeling and fashion. My runway/fashion credits included the Delta Sigma Theta Fashion show, Curvy Diva Fashion Show, Christy MUA Glam Fashion show, Vixen Style Studio, Perfect fit fashion, Fashionable Addictions, Next Level Fashion World, Modeling as a TEAM Jewel for Int. Images Biz and hosting several events myself.

Challenges: People not showing you support!

Future Accomplishments: Owning my first home

Current Challenges: I'm currently paying out of pocket tuition cost for college for my daughter. The sacrifice has been hard, but I wouldn't change it.

Short Story: Just be confident and you will succeed at whatever your heart desires.

Words of inspiration/encouragement: Just be a lady and other ladies will follow your lead! Classy never trashy!

Name: Renae Morrow

Age: 60

Occupation: IT Analyst

Fabulous Definition: Endurance under pressure, Tough, loyal caretaker… naturally maternal. Strong yet feminine, Age like no other, and most of all Resilient.

Greatest Accomplishment: Living life on my own terms. After my eldest sister passed away at 34, I realized that the female mortality rate on my mom side might not exceed the age of 40 which is the age that my mother died.

Challenges: Realizing that the female mortality rate on my mom side might not exceed the age of 40, which is the age that my mother died and family and friends telling me I should settle down and have a family.

Future Accomplishments: Absolutely, moving to another part of a country where I can live more of my life outside in the sunshine. Also, taking on a second career as an aesthetician.

Current Challenges: Making that decision on where I'd like to move to, That takes time and money but it's not anything that is going to keep me from reaching my goal.

Words of inspiration/encouragement: Life is a journey not a destination. Take time to enjoy the sights along the way!

Name: LaShon Holliday

Age: 45

Occupation: Event Planner/ Author

Greatest Accomplishment:
My greatest accomplishment thus far would be that I have completed my book Embracing your past pains!!

Challenges: The challenges that I faced while working towards my goals were that I was set up by my ex-husband and almost had to do 20 years in prison for something that I did not do. I had to have a severe brain surgery and a complete craniotomy. The doctors thought I would have to learn how to walk again and I would lose my memory.

Future Accomplishments: What I hope to accomplish in the near future is to speak to young women and share my story with them. They have possibly gone through the same thing or something similar that I have gone through. I'd like to show them how to embrace their past pains.

Current Challenges: Some of the challenges that I am facing of some kind is hard for me in reaching my goal would be somewhat financial and I'm also dealing with a family emergency.

Short Story: A short story that I would like to share on my journey to Fabulousness is never let your past hold you back from where you see yourself in the future never give up because there's always someone just waiting to hear your story and you are here to help them embrace their past pain's and Hurts so they can share their stories with others as well

Words of inspiration/encouragement: Continue to share words of inspiration and encouragement and motivation with others, continue to let your light shine, be that light that others want to see!! The Sky is not the limit it's only the beginning

Name: Traci Sogeke

Age: 52

Occupation: Travel Agent

How do you define Fabulous: A Phenomenal person that goes above and beyond... They have outstanding stamina and abilities. They are capable of virtually anything and not afraid to try harder.

Greatest Accomplishment:
I finally finished something completely. I finished the school to become a full-time Minister in the year 2000. I was able to do missionary work for two years in Mexico and teach many how to understand the Bible until recently.

Challenges: The main challenge was leaving the only culture I knew to learn a new language... Alone

Future Accomplishments: I just got married, so hope to adjust to my new husband. Along with his likes and dislikes.

Current Challenges: Yes... My greatest challenge now is to learn my new husband's customs and cultures and adapt so that I'm able to have peace at home.

Short Story: My journey started off with a loss of appreciation for my life-goals. I let a teen pregnancy propel me in another direction, not because of necessity but because of my own stupid reasoning. I married the boy next door, who in actuality was almost 10 years older than me. His mother said that he would never take care of me and my daughter. While he was in the room with us, she never addressed him and somehow I felt that I would be losing out on something great if I didn't marry him. So I did. That was by far the dumbest mistake I ever made in my life. That chapter in my life is over with... Not only is my IQ coming back up... More importantly my Common Sense has finally matured... I now know when and how to listen and take advice or direction from those qualified to give it.

Words of inspiration/encouragement: If you gain nothing else from my words... Please, take this to heart. Find a friend... Mentor if you will, from this club. Listen and learn from them. Find out how they became Fabulous. Follow the road that leads to success. It'll get you where you want to go in life much faster, and you will hit a lot less potholes along the way.

Name: Mickin S Perkins

Age: 44

Definition of Fabulous:
It starts with the inside first, the way you walk the way you talk. Fabulousness is a lifestyle

Occupation: Business Owner

Greatest Accomplishment: I consider my best accomplishment is starting over with my mind set. Getting to know me, to be a better me and the woman that I am coming to be. I like the woman in the mirror. That is my best accomplishment.

Challenges: My faith was challenged while I was working toward my goals. I forgot who I was.

Future Goals: There are a lot of things that I want to accomplish I want to get closer to God, I want to be the best wife, mother and Glamma I can be.

Current Challenges: Living knowing that I can't allow situations in life to cause me added stress.

Short Story: At the age of 36 I overcame a brain aneurysm, stroke and pulmonary embolism. My family was told that I would not regain full function and I would need a Tracheostomy and be fed through a tube. I was determined to have a full recovery and not be a burden on anyone. I went back to work the following March and singlehandedly organized the whole county jail records. No one was able to do this previously at my job. Most of the records were 20 years or more older than I am. This was a great accomplishment because I was also told I would not regain my memory.

Words of Inspiration/Encouragement: It's never too late to find the real you. Even though we are in our 40s it's not too late to learn.

Name: Dawn Singleton

Age: 42

Occupation: Cosmetologist/Business owner

How do you define Fabulous: You are Fabulous when you can make it through the toughest time in your life. Fabulousness is the strength to make it through anything.

What do you consider your greatest accomplishment is thus far: Outside of raising responsible children, I would say my greatest accomplishment is starting my own business as a black woman. I've been in business for nine years. I own a barber shop. All my booths are full. There are mostly men who work there as well as a few ladies. There are few women who own barbershops. I'm proud to say that I do.

Any challenges you may have faced while reaching your goal: I'd say financial challenges. I was able to open my own business with only $10,000. I did this on my own with no loan from the bank or anyone else.

Is there anything you hope to accomplish in the near future: I look forward to opening my second salon within this year.

Any challenges you may be facing currently while working toward your accomplishment: No
A short story you'd like to share while on your journey to fabulousness: I was a single parent raising a young man, facing financial challenges but was able to make it through with hard work and determination.

Words of inspiration/encouragement: You may mourn today but tomorrow the sun will shine and you can start all over.

Name: Deborah Falling

Age: 65

Occupation: Retired Account coordinator for Coca Cola

How do you define Fabulous: Eye catching, intelligent, poised, confident and exciting.

Greatest accomplishment: Outside of developing a relationship with God, raising my children and grandchildren to be responsible and decent human beings.

Challenges towards your accomplishment: Finding out how to maintain the proper balance between being a loving parent and a disciplinarian.

Is there anything that you hope to accomplish in the near future: I'd like to be used by Jehovah and help others to come to know him.

Short story: On my journey I realized that what I have is a lot more than what I've lost. I've lost 2 husbands, parents and three siblings. But I have also gained beautiful relationships. I have real friends. I have children that love me and I have a grandsons between the ages of 18 and 22 who are eager to spend time with me.

Words of inspiration/encouragement: Keep moving despite whatever comes up and remember that we are as Fabulous as we feel.

Name: Virginie Marie Holiday

Age: 59

Occupation: Auditor

How do you define Fabulous: God fearing, determined, a person walking in their purpose.

What do you consider your greatest accomplishment is thus far: I have connected more closely to God. I say this because all things are possible when you are connected to God, to the ones that believe.

What challenges did you face while working toward your accomplishment: One of my big challenges was facing discouragement because the things that I set out to accomplish did not quite go the way that I expected them. I also put my faith in the wrong people. I can ask God to guide me in the right direction to put the right people in my life to connect with so that I can accomplish my goals. I stepped out on faith and relied on God and his promises to me now everything is starting to fall into its place.

Is there anything you hope to accomplish in the near future: Yes, I love fashion. I plan on opening a boutique and beauty supply chain as well as invest in real estate and start my transportation business.

Are there any challenges that you are currently facing to reach your goals:
Yes, right now I am repairing my credit and healing after an injury on the job. I broke two bones in my elbow while on the job. It's been challenging getting around and doing the things that I need to do however I am doing it.

A short story you'd like to share while on your journey to fabulousness: Life is exciting and although I have challenges, I'm looking forward to what's to come. I mentioned earlier I had an accident at the job that left me injured, however I'm still encouraged and motivated. As I'm healing, I'm putting total faith in God and I have the confidence that things will work out according to his will.

Words of inspiration/encouragement: Always keep God before you. Anything that you do, step out on faith, trust, believe and know that God will work out whatever you need to do or want to do in life. Never give up on your dreams. Sometimes you might get discouraged and feel like what's to come is not going to come but just keep God before you. Walk in faith, believe and know that whatever dream you have inside of you, you can bring it out through the grace of God.

Name: Catherine Roberson

Age: 51

Occupation: Housewife

Definition of Fabulous: Compassionate, empathetic, loving and forgiving. Being forgiving is Fabulous.

Accomplishment: Outside of solidifying my relationship with Jehovah I would say marrying my best friend is my greatest accomplishment.

Challenges: Being unsure of myself and being insecure led to jealousy. I was able to overcome my insecurity as I grew older and learned that everything is not that serious. Life works itself out

Is there anything that you hope to accomplish in the near future: Every day is an adventure for me. My husband has given me the marriage of my dreams. I have great friends. And I'm confident that whatever life has in store I will succeed and overcome any challenge.

Short story: One thing I've learned is everyone needs a confidant and don't ever betray their trust. Keep your friends secrets close to your heart. I have friends that tell me so many things and many times I'm just their listening ear.

Words of inspiration/encouragement: Life is not fair but it's still good. I love that quote. I don't remember where I will read it, but I found it to be so true.

Name: Bonnie Jones

Age: 67

Occupation: Administrative Assistant

How do you define fabulous: Confident, optimistic and spiritual.

What do you consider your greatest accomplishment thus far: Being a mentor to young people.

What challenges did you face while working toward your goal: Trying to be a good listener and having empathy for others circumstances and having patience has been my challenges.

Is there anything you hope to accomplish in the near future: I want to always be a source of encouragement to others. That's what I'd like to accomplish. I'd like to leave this earth knowing that I've had a positive influence on someone.

Any challenges you may be facing while working toward this: Keeping my mouth shut, knowing when to speak and when not to speak and not being so opinionated.

A short story you'd like to share while on your journey to fabulousness: I was in a situation where I had to mentor a young person who quit high school. I had to learn to be understanding, patient, considerate and firm. This young lady now is doing well. She got back into school and graduated. Now she has an Associates degree. She found out that she loves school and she's much more outgoing and confidant. To know I played a part in this brings me great joy and a sense of accomplishment.

Words of inspiration/encouragement: Be true to yourself. Believe in yourself. Set boundaries of behavior on how you want to be treated.

Name: Vickie Beals

Age: 50

Occupation: Fire Department Chief

Fabulous Definition:
My definition of Fabulous is a woman that Stands during the biggest Storm of her life. Recognizing the new devil with each of her new levels and knowing that Empowered Women Empower Others.

Greatest Accomplishment:
My Greatest accomplishment is being Friends as well as a Parent with my 17 year old daughter.

Current Challenges: Working in a male-dominated industry as an African-American Woman. Having a voice, opinions, industry knowledge and being a thinker, can cultivate an environment of sexism, racism and inferiority complexities. The challenge is to maintain the courage not to quit.

Future Goals: I hope to accomplish in the near future being a part of preparing and educating young African-American men and women for the emergency medical services/fire service industry and assisting them to participate in the hiring process for this city's fire department. I am obligated to give back and help these kids reach their goals and give back to the very efforts of those who gave to me.

Future Challenges: I am currently finalizing a very difficult divorce, protecting my daughter from the darkness of this process, relocating, mentoring future EMS/Fire Young Women and Men and preparing for a pending promotion at work, all while I fight violence in the work place and sexual harassment on my job by a superior officer has its challenges.

Short Story:
What Satan meant for my distraction got turned into a triumph. One day I arrived home only to find that the locks on my home had been changed by my husband. There are no words to express the hurt, fear and betrayal I felt at that very moment my key didn't work to my home of 15 years. My teenage daughter sat in the car in devastation as I had to come back and explain to her that I needed to get the police to help us get back into the house. But God! The spirit Spoke to me and said do not fight to go back into the space that God removed you from! It was at that time, at that moment, I started a new life. The life I've always wanted... living in the place I've always wanted to live. I've always had a connection to water. I have always known that I wanted to wake

up every morning looking at God's glory... God's beautiful blessing, water. The confirmation was when my 17-year-old said to me, "Mom I want to live near water". Yes, I was initially afraid to step out on faith but that lasted a half a second... Then I knew after a split second that it was time for me to step into my Fabulousness and the life I really deserved for me and my child...

Words of inspiration/encouragement:
New Levels create New Devils.... Create a Good Day for yourself....

Name: Terry Cole

Age: 58

Occupation: Substitute teacher/ Basketball Official

Definition of Fabulous: Remaining Strong despite obstacles and life. Continually working toward reaching goals

Greatest Accomplishment thus far: I consider my greatest accomplishment is raising my children to adulthood while continuously working and striving to be the best me in mind, body and soul.

Challenges: I overcame many trials and tribulations that could have altered my path, had I succumbed to the temptations.

Future Accomplishments: I am working to become debt free, if possible.

Current Challenges: Well I'm trying to help my children become totally independent financially so they can stay out of my back pocket.

Short Story: I didn't really grow up until I lost my mother who was my best friend. I felt loss and alone even though I have a wonderful husband whom I have learned to totally lean on for strength and courage to go forward through my difficult loss.

Words of inspiration/encouragement: Put God first!

Name: Karen Delaney

Age: 51

Occupation: Store Manager

My definition of FABULOUS:
F is for Fabulous
A is for Amazing
B is for Beautiful
U is for Unique
L is for Loved
O if for Outgoing
U is for Unbothered
S is for Serene/Serenity
To sum FABULOUS up in a nutshell, you are who
you make yourself out to be. Beauty is skin deep.
One will have to be comfortable with her own skin
to know that there are more ways than one of being
FABULOUS

Greatest Accomplishment thus far: My greatest
accomplishment has been raising five sons as a full-
time MOM, working a full-time job, and obtaining
three Degrees within 8 years.

Challenges: My challenges were having to wear
many hats and shift my mindset to be able to

function and operate efficiently while being away from home to ensure my sons were disciplined in a manner to keep them out of trouble.

Future Accomplishments: My future goals are simple, such as starting my own business, becoming a homeowner, and networking with people to gain knowledge while on the road to financial freedom.

Current Challenges: My recent challenge has been time management. I had to learn that it's extremely important to set time out for SELF.

Short Story: On my journey to FABULOUSNESS, I'm looking forward to living my BEST LIFE. What that means for me is surrounding myself with Fabulous women who share the same aspirations as I do. I have made a commitment that I will live my life free of stress, negativity, and toxic people. I'm at the age where it is essential for me to have a PEACE OF MIND.

Words of inspiration/encouragement: My words of encouragement; You control your own happiness. Often times in life, we partake in many different things that really have no significant meaning or effect pertaining to our own good health. I would say that if you're not happy about a situation, only YOU

CAN MAKE THAT CHANGE. Control what you can and change what you cannot, it's called SERENITY. Live, Love, & Laugh is my key to a healthy lifestyle.

Name: Sheila Saffold

Age: 58

Occupation: Retired Accountant for the Federal Government. Currently a retail merchant

Fabulous Definition: A person who knows themselves and their worth and is dedicated to doing their best in life.

Greatest Accomplishment thus far: Being able to show my children the value of being dedicated and focused on something they are passionate about as well as showing them how to appreciate the quality of life while being responsible.

Challenges: Being able to take control of my own responsibilities and realizing what I put out is what I will receive. Learning humility.

Future Accomplishments: To attain more peace and be able to listen to the guidance of God more.

Short Story: My stepfather told me that no matter what I experienced or who my biological father was I would always be loved by him. He told me I was his child and to never seek the love of someone who doesn't accept you for who you are. That was my first experience of true love from a man and it really meant everything to me.

Words of inspiration/encouragement: 1st have respect for yourself, in order for others to have respect for you. As you grow into adulthood you will go through stages of maturity, reflect back and learn from past experiences. Also listen to God, He has a plan for you.

Name: Danielle Dickerson

Age: 50

Occupation: Educator

Fabulous Definition: Fabulous is strong, determined, motivated and God fearing

Greatest Accomplishment thus far: My greatest accomplishment is graduating from college with honors as a single mother of two young children and a widow.

Challenges: I became homeless with my children because my ex-husband was on drugs. I made the decision to leave him and go to college, taking my children with me. I attended college without any help during the first three years. I took my children to school with me, studying late nights while my children slept, and worked part-time. I graduated with honors and a Masters degree. I bought property, got re-married, bought additional pieces of properties, went back to school and got my specialist in leadership and am a business owner.

Future Accomplishments: In the near future, I will continue to educate young people and build a future on touching lives.

Current Challenges: I want to open a charter school for students who can't make it in a public school setting. My challenges are finding a building location and necessary paperwork to start.

Short Story: On the road to Fabulousness, keep God first and stay the course.

Words of inspiration/encouragement: God must be first in your life. It's important to set goals and keep them.

Name: Donna R. Guy

Age: 55

Occupation: Business Administrator

Fabulous Definition: A Fabulous person always strives to accomplish their goals no matter what age and stage in life. They are confident and Motivating

Greatest Accomplishment: I wouldn't say it's my greatest but I'm mighty proud of myself for returning to school after a lengthy absence and earning an MBA at the age of 53.

Challenges: Time management, dedication and the support of family proved to be challenging during that time. There were many times I wanted to give up but there was always that voice in the background telling me to continue. I knew what I was capable of and had to ignore the naysayers in order to achieve my goal.

Future Accomplishments: I love learning and earning a PhD would be icing on the cake! I won't rule it out in the future.

Current Challenges: None that I can think of at the moment.

Short Story: After working 18 years in the telecommunications industry I found myself unemployed when my position was downsized. At that time, I was an adult learner working towards an undergraduate degree in Business. I decided to make a career change to an area that was more secure. I now have an MBA in Human Resources and Training and Development. I find working as an HR Professional to be very rewarding, gratifying and gives me that work-life balance that I've always wanted.

Words of inspiration/encouragement: Never stop learning! Never quit! Do the things that make you happy!

Name: Tasha k

Age: 43

Fabulous Definition: a person who knows what they want in life, who's confident, determined and sexy

Occupation: Customer services rep

Greatest Accomplishment: 1) Raising three kids as a single mom, (2 kids finished college). 2) buying my first home in 2011, 3) staying stable while being on my job for 16yrs

Challenges: Raising my oldest son in the city of Chicago, trying to keep him from the streets and keep him safe was my biggest challenge, but we got thru it.

Future Accomplishments: Yes, getting married soon. And buying a family building

Current Challenges: No

Short Story: My journey as a Fabulous woman is that I'm a mother, a fiancé, a homeowner, friend, lover, and strong woman who works very hard in staying happy and sexy

Words of inspiration/encouragement: God is the head of all Our lives, give him the praise for waking you up this morning, thank him for giving you the skills and gift to accomplish your goals. God is your healing, but you are the person responsible for your Own happiness. Keep your head up and a smile on your face! No matter what obstacle comes your way.

Name: Onika Brown

Age: 41

Occupation: Esthetician

Fabulous Definition: Understanding your power and purpose

Greatest Accomplishment: My greatest accomplishment thus far has been to have the courage to follow my dreams and maintain the faith needed to manifest having my own salon.

Challenges: Mainly, the challenges that I faced were financial. Just the ability to gain resources to keep things together.

Future Accomplishments: In the near future, I look forward to helping young women understand their power and how to tap into their purpose.

Current Challenges: Currently, the challenges I am facing is the ability to stay motivated outside my circumstances and lack of resources.

Short Story: Recently, I lost my mother. My best friend. Grieving has taken a toll on my health and mental. Although, I can hear her say that Doll face Cosmetics will be great. I still struggle with being sure. So, I have decided to do some inner spiritual work and get the motivation I need to press forward to Fabulousness.

Words of inspiration/encouragement: Everything you need is ALREADY inside of you. God has given us all that we need.

Name: Ronda Lake

Age: 46

Occupation: Designator Hitter

Fabulous Definition: A person who can push through life's storm and maintain their faith

Greatest Accomplishment: My greatest accomplishment thus far, finishing college with my degree in Applied Science, giving birth to my beautiful daughter and most of all being honest with myself about my past, which is allowing me to make better decisions in life.

Challenges: While working toward my goals I was face with the voices of my deceased stepfather saying I would never amount to anything, being a single mother, the loss of my sister passing of cervical cancer, moving from my partner's place of residency not once but twice, I felt abandoned by my biological father and through all this I survived Arnold Chiari-Malformation (brain surgery).

Future Accomplishments: In my near future my faith will be stronger. I will have a house for my daughter and myself, become a licensed technician, and help those that are in need.

Current Challenges: At this time, I'm learning how to build my faith in The Lord. My Finances are in need of an increase.

Short Story: Keep God First in my life and my family as well. Removing all negativity from my spirit. Speaking only positive words from my mouth.

Words of inspiration/encouragement: Get to know God for yourself and always put The Lord First, Nevertheless!

Name: Darlene Houston

Age: 59

Occupation: Office Manager/Direct Support
Professional

Definition of Fabulous: Self Confidence,

Greatest Accomplishment: Overcoming the
negative effects of foster care, and a parent who
suffered from mental illness.

Challenges: Overcoming the fear of considering
myself as an asset to self and others.

Future Accomplishments: Yes, living a life of total
and complete contentment!

Current Challenges: I am not dealing with any
specific challenges, other than the ones that come
financially, but I still have not reached all of my
goals.

Words of inspiration/encouragement: Don't be
afraid to dream! Allow yourself to fly. With arms
stretched high, reach out far enough and hard enough
for your dreams, until you attain them!

Name: Michelle Wicks

Age: 53

Occupation: Fleet service Clerk & Bible Student

Fabulous Definition: When I think of Fabulous my definition might be slightly different from the dictionary. I know the dictionary defines Fabulous as extra-ordinary, outstanding and exceptional and that is very true. Fabulous to me is a beauty that's within. Someone who is warm and loving. Someone who is caring and not just in word but also in deed. A Fabulous person to me is God fearing, puts Jehovah first, has love for neighbor as they have love themselves. Also, a Fabulous person is unique and displays unique qualities.

A Fabulous person has the ability to multitask, has special talents, and knows how to acquire special skills. A Fabulous person is someone who you can communicate well with.

A Fabulous person is someone who is amazing, always looking to say or do something good & that's what Fabulous is to me.

Greatest Accomplishment: Having a relationship with Jehovah God, Baptism, giving birth to 4 children that all completed school and now have families of their own, starting over from rock bottom, rebuilding my credit and purchasing a home on my own, being on my job long term,

Challenges: Opposition of baptism, jealousy, negativity, starting over from rock bottom, multi-tasking, work, spiritual goals, home life, & rebuilding my credit has all been a challenge.

Future Accomplishments: Retirement, to be a better Bible student, better teacher, better researcher, better friend

Current Challenges: Financial obligations of 3 households, looking out for mom, trying to multi-task my time. I'm too young to retire and family is pulling me in all different directions.

Short Story: Get back up again. No matter how many stumbling blocks that appear in your path keep getting up. Remember what Jesus went through, what Job endured and remember there are many worse off than we are. Trust in Jehovah with your whole heart and you can move mountains.

Words of inspiration/encouragement: When life feeds you lemons, make lemonade. Love intently from the heart and always speak consolingly to depressed souls.

Name: Valerie Marie Furr-Collins

Age: 45

Occupation: Businesswoman/Blogger/Writer

Fabulous Definition: Fabulous is always doing your best despite challenges

Greatest Accomplishment: My greatest accomplishment(s) are my two children. They have truly been my lifelines in my darkest moments. My greatest professional accomplishment was graduating LPN school at the top of my class regardless of adversity.

Challenges: My biggest challenge I faced was being diagnosed with fibromyalgia at the young age of 22 years old. I was forced to leave RN school and the diagnoses completely changed the course of my life.

Future Accomplishments: I have so many things I hope to accomplish in the future. First, I want to publish my first book by October 2019. That's the deadline I have given myself. I wish to complete my Bachelor's degree in Healthcare Management so that I can do what I set out to do in nursing 20 plus years ago, teach the profession I love.

Current Challenges: My biggest challenge is the current state of my health. Some days a better than others but I have let Fibromyalgia stop me for way too long. Another challenge, to be honest, is I'm not financially sound. I've been on disability since 2001. I have not been able to sustain employment due to my health refusing to cooperate, but I've never stopped trying. Another challenge is balancing my time. I struggle to balance my time between my goals, caring for my wonderful mother, my older brother, my six-year-old twin niece and nephew, my crochet business, and writing my books, blog posts, and poetry. But it gets easier every day.

Short Story: I had a difficult childhood, but I've always been close to my mother, who is my heart. When my father fell ill (comatose) following surgery in 1993, my mother gave the six of us children life for a second time. See, my father had some undiagnosed issues. He kept us girls under lock and key. He loved us, but I understand he was sick. After my dad didn't wake up, my mother didn't make us stay locked up, she set us free to make a life for ourselves in this world. She supported us then and supports us now. My father lived 16 1/2 years in a vegetative state. We lost him on his 68th birthday, March 13, 2009. We would go on to lose my oldest brother that June 2009 and my grandfather that December 2009. Three generations gone but never forgotten.

Words of inspiration/encouragement: Do your best until you know better. When you know better, do better! ~Dr. Maya Angelou

Name: A.P.

Age: 52

Occupation: Public safety

Fabulous Definition: Being Fabulous is always improving oneself

Greatest Accomplishment: I feel my greatest accomplishments are my daughter's accomplishments. Seeing her excel in her studies, her goals with morals and value.

Challenges: My challenge was people not believing that I could do it.

Future Accomplishments: I'm looking forward to starting my own business and a non-profit to give back to the community I live in.

Current Challenges: Just that people think you aren't capable of change...God's peace on my life keeps me going....

Short Story: After I had my daughter, my whole life changed. I found a church and joined. My spirituality is my foundation. And that is why I am who I am today. Am I perfect? No. But I am not trying to judge, hurt or get over on anyone.

Words of inspiration/encouragement: This world we live in is tough. You cannot do it by yourself. Find a church that is a good fit for you and watch your life forever change.

Name: Brenda Fairley-Williams

Age: 67

Occupation: Retired Verizon communications supervisor. Actress, business owner, motivational mentor

How do you define Fabulous: Fabulousness is within, being happy with you. In order to be Fabulous you must be happy with yourself

What do you consider your greatest accomplishment: Helping others and hearing how I inspired their life.

Any challenges while reaching your goal: Talking (back then) networking, always trying to better myself so that I may in help others better themselves

Future goals: Being a successful actress.

Current challenges: I don't let things get to me like other people. I'm going through the average things that any actor or actress will go through while working toward being successful.

Short story: I have great faith and I'm a computer

person that has helped to diminish stress in my life while I'm reaching my ultimate goals.

Words of inspiration/encouragement: Be true to yourself. Find out who you are. Always know you can work on becoming a better you.

Name: Pearlene Haralson

Age:83

Occupation: Retired Field service manager for the Board of Education in Chicago and a retired CAN

How do you define Fabulous: When you think positive and know how to take care of yourself, maintaining your look, when you're healthy and have a good personality, also having faith in God is Fabulous.

What is your greatest accomplishment thus far: Surviving, living a long life and having most of what I want.

Any challenges faced while meeting your accomplishment: Having to build on my own needs. I had a husband for 45 years six children and I provided for them with no public assistance.

Words of inspiration/encouragement: Stay positive, be honest and put God first in your life and have a goals for your life.

Name: Arvella Wilcox

Age: 52

Occupation: Consultant

How do you define Fabulous: Myself, being authentic

What do you consider your greatest accomplishment thus far: Becoming a mother of three children that have proven to be responsible and self-sufficient.

Any challenges while reaching that accomplishment: Never giving up and letting my children know without failure you will never know your greatest strength

Anything you look to accomplish in the near future: Becoming a well-rounded woman of God

Current Challenges: Staying faithful and knowing that the path God has me on is going to be a journey also knowing his direction will lead me to becoming the well-rounded woman of God that I want to be.

A short story while on your journey to fabulousness: I continued to believe in myself. I told myself I was beautiful regardless of whatever, so no matter whatever I encountered I was able to persevere which has led me to my authentic self.

Words of encouragement/inspiration: Regardless what life roles you, just believe that you can and know that you can and you will.

Name: Earlene Estelle

Age: 80

Occupation: Nurse school teacher

How do you define Fabulous: A person who is considerate of others. Someone who is a hard worker, giving and caring, someone who likes to have fun, a well-rounded person.

What do you consider your greatest accomplishment thus far: Reaching the age of almost 81.

Any challenges that you overcame will while reaching your goal: Being married to my husband for 46 years. Growing up with spirituality because things were challenging during that time. Just getting money to get my degree during that time was hard work. Working and taking care of a child while going to school these all were a challenge.

Anything you look to accomplish in the near future: No, just aging gracefully.

Inspiration/encouragement: You can accomplish anything you want to if you want it bad enough.

Name: Ruby Leeason

Age:76

Occupation: Retired security receptionist.

How do you define Fabulous: Feeling good about yourself no matter what you look like or what you're doing. As long as you are being your own person, you are fabulous.

What do you consider your greatest accomplishment: Loving people is my greatest accomplishment and having a great personality. Showing love accomplishes a lot.

Any challenges: Holding onto true friendships.

Anything you look to accomplish in the near future: Living my life. As long as I'm alive I never want to sit still and do nothing.

Any story that you can share of something you accomplish to overcome that will encourage the next: I always had speech problems since the time that I was born. I still have them, but I overcame the fact that I wouldn't be able to say certain words or pronounce certain names. The words I didn't know or couldn't say, I found an alternative to use that would work as best as possible. I did not let that bother me. I overcame it and I grew confidence through my experiences with people and because of that, I met and communicated with people from all around the world including Prince Charles and many other dignitaries.

Words of inspiration/encouragement: Be nice to people. Every once in a while, people are going to be nasty but just be nice and to be yourself.

Name: Virgie Williams

Age: 74

Occupation: Retired Nurse

How do you define Fabulousness: Fabulous is fine and being yourself.

What do you consider your greatest accomplishment thus far: Raising my children has been my greatest accomplishment. I love my kids

Any challenges you faced while working toward your accomplishment: I have six children. Raising them to be responsible had its challenges. Losing a child that was mental and physical handicapped was a major challenge that still affects me today but I got through it.

Anything you work towards accomplishing in the near future: Living a long healthy life and enjoying my children.

Story: I was diagnosed with a brain tumor a little over a year ago. It was originally the size of a quarter and within four months it shrunk down to the size of a dime. I was grateful to God that they did not have to operate on me.

Words of inspiration/encouragement: Don't work harder work smarter.

Name: Janis Dunn

Age: 60

Occupation: Claims Director

How do you define Fabulous: Fabulousness is more of a mindset on how confident you are in being yourself in whatever state that you're in.

What do you consider your greatest accomplishment the far: Becoming president of the tri-city NAACP.

There any challenges you may have faith while working toward your accomplishment: There is always rejection when you are Type A personality. When you have strong ideas and a direct path to how to get there, people sometime reject that.

Anything you like to accomplish in the near future: I would like to have success in my new position, enhance economic development within the community and build stronger relationships with community partners

Any challenges you may be encountering thus far: Filling all the roles of various different

committees of the unit with qualified individuals.
People tend to take roles because of the title and the
recognition that it may come with, but they may not
be qualified.

**A short story while on your journey toward
fabulousness:** I decided to become a yoga instructor
about three years ago to overcome physical
challenges, build a better mindset regarding self-
esteem and being mindful of others around me. My
business has grown, and I am instructing various
different organizations, fraternities, sororities and
local doctor offices on wellness.

Words of inspiration/encouragement: Always
trust God. I think of Jeremiah 29:11 that God has a
plan for each and every one of us, that's for us to
prosper and that doesn't necessarily mean materially
or financially but to prosper in the mind, body and
spirit of Christ

Name: Rosie Day

Age: 65

Occupation: Retired city of Atlanta employee and continuing caregiver for special need adults.

How do you define Fabulous: Self-confidence

What do you consider your greatest accomplishment thus far: Having become a well-rounded, sensible and sensitive human being.

Any challenges you face to achieve your greatest accomplishment: Being understood, communicating properly with others.

Anything you look forward to accomplishing in the near future: Being more grounded spiritually and helping those in other countries through philanthropy.

Any challenges you're currently facing to reach your future accomplishment: Maintaining good health

Our short story that you can share while on your journey to fabulousness that may encourage the next: I've overcome three divorces in my life and lived to retire comfortably despite life's hurdles. I've been able be a strong backbone and support to my children. I'm proud to be who I am and where I am in life.

Words of inspiration/encouragement: Always recognize and put God first in everything that you do. Always be mindful of God and all you're doing.

Name: Elberstine Bean

Age: 90

Occupation: Retired Beautician

How do you define fabulous: Successful, outgoing, confident and a people person.

What do you think your greatest accomplishment is thus far: I have been a stronghold for my family and I was also able to be a caretaker for my brother for 20 years until he died at the age of 70.

Any challenges you incurred while reaching your accomplishment: My brother was born severely handicapped. His lifespan according to the doctors was 15 years, but he lived until the age of 70. He couldn't talk, he couldn't walk, he was an infant his whole life. It was a challenge taking care of him, but I was truly proud of being able to. He lived past 15 years until 70 and I played a big part in that. I took care of him. He outlived most of our family members. Five sisters and two brothers except me and the last 20 years of his life, it was just him and I. And when he died, I was holding his hand. We slept alongside of each other. His bed and my bed, right next to one another and when I think about him now,

I just smile.

Anything you would like to accomplish in the near future: I would like to go out more and have a share in the door to door ministry because I'm one of Jehovah's Witnesses. I was unable to take a share as I wanted to because of my responsibilities. Now I'm able to take a fuller share in telling others about God's kingdom, this is a public service.

Any challenges I'm currently face while working toward my future goal: I'm dealing with heart and health issues which limits my share in door to door ministry.

A short story of challenges you overcome while on your journey to fabulousness: My husband was a business owner for many years. He owned a mechanic shop on Roosevelt Road. He would repair, detail and deliver cars. His was the only shop like that within miles. During both Martin Luther King riots his business was demolished along with all the other businesses on Roosevelt and he suffered a severe stroke. This made me step up and become the financial backbone of the family. I got a job as a salesperson and it kept us together. I also became a beautician and I took care of my husband until his death. I'm proud to say I was able to financially sustain my family and be a backbone to them over the years.

Words of inspiration/encouragement: When faced with a situation step up to the plate, give it all you've got and you will succeed. It worked for me!

BONUS

Name: Lisa Moore

Age: Fabulous and 40+

Small Checklist to begin with:
Life is short and it's what you make it.
Remember to take deep breathes from the bottom of your stomach.
Be nice and kill'em with kindness.
Ignore negative behaviors that don't concern you and yours.
Help the young'ns in any way you can.
Makeup is your friend.
It's enough "Sexy to go around!"
Don't be jealous!

CHAPTER 9

JOURNEY TO TRUE FABULOUSNESS

Let's go over some of the key things mentioned in this book that we can use as a compass and map on our journey to Fabulousness.

Number one: What we feel is Fabulous can have an impact on our current and future lives.

Number two: Our view of Fabulosity begins to take shape at a very early age and is affected by our surroundings and upbringing.

Number three: Statistics show by the age 40, most of us have reached a higher level of maturity (this is not always the case, this also does not mean that some of us don't feel as if we can use direction after 40).

Number four: The generation that each of us were

born in has a large effect on how we interact through life.

Number five: Ideals and values have changed over time and not necessarily for the better.

Number six: What is important or not important to us now, will have an impact on our children either for the good or bad.

Number seven: Many now have the wrong idea of what it truly means to be Fabulous.

Number eight: I had to say something because we need more role models. The future of our society is in desperate need of up and coming positive role models and influencers.

Number nine: Each of us must do all we can to help younger ones avoid life's potholes and understand what true Fabulousness is.

Number 10: Inspiration is the key!

Please reflect on the stories you just read and remember these key points. Answer the questions for yourself. Think about your future goals. Jot down any words or thoughts that you can to inspire the next.

Name:

Age:

How do I define the word Fabulous:

What do I consider my greatest accomplishment is thus far:

What challenge have I faced while working toward that accomplishment:

Is there anything I hope to accomplish in the near future:

Are there any challenges I am currently facing to reach the goal I'm working toward:

A journal of my story:

Words of encouragement and inspiration that I can share:

CHAPTER 10

THE FUTURE OF F.A.B

Accessory Me (and its affiliates), the Fabulous 40 & Over Club (and its members) and myself personally would like you to be involved in the future of your FAB. You can do this by participating and supporting (when you can) the upcoming FAB Project events.

The purpose of The FAB (Fierce and Beautiful) Project is to support women (young and old) in proactively working toward their financial freedom and educate them on inner and outer beauty. This program is for all, but especially for those who are dealing with challenging circumstances.

The FAB Project along with its affiliates will offer entrepreneurship education and resources to those who participate in our programs. We will also offer self-esteem and positive role model courses as well as makeup and beauty classes to those in school and in shelters. We will pick a shelter each month to donate self-care/beauty packages to. We are looking forward to a yearly Business & Beauty summit and we would like to invite you and your voice to be heard.

Let's do our best to inspire the rest!

Join our email list and feel free to share your story or words of advice at www.fabulous40andoverclub.com